GRACE FOR THE RACE

MINDY ROSS

*But they who wait for the Lord shall renew
their strength; they shall mount up with
wings like eagles; they shall run and not be
weary; they shall walk and not faint.*
—Isaiah 40:31 (ESV)

ACKNOWLEDGMENTS

Jesus! Anything good that comes from me, ultimately comes from Him! Thank you Heavenly Father for your unending grace, and the call you have placed upon my life.

Grandma Georgia—I promised you another book, so you can stop reading *Finding Strength*. In all seriousness, you gave me the motivation to keep writing when I wanted to quit. I love you.

Jus—My man, my hero, and the love of my life. God knew I would need a strong, confident man to push me to pursue His purpose for me. I am so thankful for your support and guidance, and your biceps.

Kids—Kaden, you're a stud. You changed my life forever when you came into this world. Mckenzie, you are the sweetest person I know. I don't know what I did to deserve such a great kid. Temperance-girl, you have a great purpose in this life. You connect to people in a way that most can't, and you've taught me more than you know. Isabella, AKA "Peanut," I love you to the moon and back, twice. Please stay silly, keep making messes, and never stop laughing. Child in my belly, I can't wait to meet you, squeeze you, and be your mommy. I hope you are ready to be a part of this crazy family!

Dad and Mom—Thanks for the spankin's. I'm kidding. I love and respect you two more than you know for building our family on faith in Jesus, and loving us sacrificially and unconditionally.

Cara—My sis. I know the love of God because of you. You know everything about me. You've seen me at my worst, and you loved me through it all. You know my weaknesses, but you always applaud my strengths. You're the best sister a girl could ever ask for, and one of God's greatest gifts to me. Love you.

Hey friends! Mindy here, and I am pumped that you are joining me on this journey to living a grace-filled life in a stressed-out world! We all have a race to run, and we need the grace of God to finish it!

You will get to know me a little more throughout this book, but you should know up front that I love humor, food, and funny things, and chocolate, and did I already say food? Anyway, I pray this book will be like a pep talk from your crazy (but very spiritual) best friend. If I could take a peek into your life, I bet I would see a strong person who has been through some stuff, and lived to tell about it. A person who is running a race, but gets a little tired sometimes, and a person who wants to make a difference, but could use a little encouragement now and then. That's what *Grace for the Race* is here for.

So, what are we waiting for? Lace up your kicks (or keep them off; it's just a metaphor), and let's run this race together!

TABLE OF CONTENTS

CHAPTERS

GOD'S GRACE, YOUR SUPERPOWER

CHAPTER 1

*But they who wait for the Lord shall renew
their strength; they shall mount up with wings
like eagles; they shall run and not be weary;
they shall walk and not faint.*
—Isaiah 40:31 (ESV)

If you could have any superpower, what would it be? I've always wanted
to fly. I'm not the bird-watching type, but every now and then, while
sitting on my back deck with a cup of coffee in hand, I'll spend
some time watching in amazement as birds of all types soar across my
backyard. Some of them fly hastily, like they've got somewhere to be;
some fly playfully, flirting with one another; and some fly gracefully, as
if they haven't a care in the world. If I'm honest, they make me jealous.
Sometimes I wish I could just put some distance between myself and
my surroundings and soar through the clouds for a bit, letting the wind
block out the many noises of this chaotic life. In fact, any time I am
on a flight, I sit by the window so I can watch the world get smaller
and smaller. My favorite part of the flight is when we surpass the cloud
barrier, and regardless of what's going on below, it's always sunny above

the clouds. There could be rain, fog, storms, or snow in Columbus, but once we break through the clouds, it's all sun. If I could choose any selfish superpower, I would fly.

When I think of God's grace, I see it as God's superpower that He offers to each of His children. To each person, it is revealed differently, but one thing is the same for all of us: **God's grace is His supernatural empowerment that enables us to do what we couldn't on our own.** It is an undeserved, unearned gift from our Heavenly Father that equips us for this life. It is by His grace that we can be good moms and dads. It is by His grace that we perform in our careers at a level we couldn't naturally. It is by His grace that we love others who are difficult to love. It is by His grace that we persevere through the trials of life and don't lose heart. In fact, God gives us a beautiful illustration in the book of Isaiah of what life lived within God's grace looks like:

> *But they who wait for the Lord shall renew*
> *their strength; they shall mount up with wings*
> *like eagles; they shall run and not be weary;*
> *they shall walk and not faint.—Isaiah 40:31*

When you are living within the grace of God, it doesn't mean you won't face storms in life. It means that you will have the strength and power to soar through the storms of life. Your strength will be renewed each day, and God's grace will be sufficient in your times of trouble.

GRACE MULTIPLIED

Throughout the New Testament, we read the words "grace and peace" in introductions from Apostle Paul, the letters of Peter, and the writings of John. It is clear that these two things go together. Grace and peace. When we are living by the grace of God, we have access to a peace that surpasses our own understanding. We can walk through the darkest valleys, and maintain our faith. We can get a shut-off notice from the electric company, and remain joyful. We can be in the midst of a volatile relationship and still have love for that person. How is that possible? Because God's grace isn't given just one time. It is measured out to you in the amount that you need for the season.

> *May grace and peace be multiplied to you in*
> *the knowledge of God and of Jesus our Lord.*
> —*2 Peter 1:2*

Peter makes it clear that we don't just get one dose of grace. Grace can be multiplied when we need it. And in February of 2011, boy, did I need it.

NOT THE MAMA!

Maybe I've dated myself with that quote from the old Dinosaur sitcom, where the little baby always calls his daddy by the title, "Not the Mama." That's what I was for a little baby girl who needed a mom in 2011.

I was six months pregnant when I received a text that a little girl had been born in my extended family and needed a home immediately, or she would be sent to foster care. We prayed, God spoke, and we decided to take her in.

Thus began the year of crazy. We were crazy to take in a newborn when we were pregnant with our third. We were crazy to try to fit four kids into an 900-square-foot home. We were crazy to think we could provide for them when we could barely keep the heat on every month. We were crazy to think we could work full-time, volunteer in the church, start a business, and care for all these little humans. We were crazy. People told us that, and they were right. It was the craziest year of my life so far. Looking back, I honestly don't know how I survived. I remember caring for Temperance during those last four months of my pregnancy, taking her in for her weekly check-ups, and also taking her to my weekly pregnancy check-ups. I remember holding two newborns, one on each knee, while I sat cross-legged, a bottle in each hand. I remember carrying two car seats everywhere we went, while still keeping an eye on my toddlers. I don't know how I did it, but for the grace of God.

It was the grace of God that helped me not only survive that season physically and mentally, but also have the capacity to care for others through it. You see, when we took in Temperance, we also took on the full weight of the case, including her biological parents. We prayed for them daily. We encouraged them to get help so they could see their daughter. And then we did something radical. We started bringing them to church. Every Sunday for six months, we would drive into the inner city, pick them up from wherever they were, and bring them to church. I would hand over Temperance to her birth mom for the service, in hopes that it would give her the motivation she needed to change. Sadly, that didn't happen soon enough. At nine months, we were given full custody of their daughter, and we stopped hearing from them for a while.

For the next four years, we continued to pray protection over her mother, wherever she was. Every now and then we would get word that she was still alive, which was relieving because we knew the severity of her condition. We had lost contact with her, but we didn't lose faith.

A MEXICAN FIESTA

In March 2017, we received a phone call from Tempie's mom. She was one year clean, married, and pursuing her GED! Justin and I were overjoyed. We met her for lunch at our favorite Mexican restaurant, and over some chicken and queso, we cried, we laughed, and we caught each other up on what had happened over the last four years. She had been to hell and back with her addiction to heroin. She almost died twice from overdoses. But she met a man who made it his mission to help her. She was enrolled in classes, attending church every Sunday, and participating in Narcotics Anonymous meetings five times a week. As she sat across the table, I heard the words, "I'm sorry" for the first time. In that moment, we gave her the greatest gift we could— forgiveness. I pulled out some pictures of Tempie from my purse. Justin and I shared some memories we had with her, we talked about her personality, and we left her with a few photographs to keep for herself. That day we saw the fruition of years of prayer.

Now, Temperance has what we had always hoped for—a relationship with her birth mom. She sees her on holidays and birthdays, and enjoys playdates with her now and then. I give all the credit to God for His amazing grace that got us through the hardest season of our lives, and gave her mother a brand-new life!

If it weren't for His grace, I know without a doubt that we would not have handled that season well. We couldn't have survived it mentally, physically, or emotionally. We may have gotten so tired and frustrated that we couldn't pray for Tempie's mom. We may not have sacrificed our time and energy to drive into Columbus to pick her up for church every Sunday. We may not have picked up the phone when she called. And we may not have had the ability to forgive.

I look back on 2011 in awe of God's grace. It's a time I would never want to relive, because I'm not sure how I survived it. But it is a time I am forever grateful to God for. Today, our life is 180 degrees different. It's much slower paced. We can actually pay all our bills. We don't live in fear of shut-off notices. We have the house we always wanted and two working vehicles. God has blessed us. That doesn't mean we don't face trials, but I know the same grace that got us through 2011 will get us through every year after.

GET YOURS

Are you going through something in life that is so heavy, so difficult, that you know you won't be able to handle it on your own? Are you in that crazy season of life, and you're not sure how you're going to survive? Are you getting weary in doing good things and always being the strong one?

Here is some encouragement for you: the same grace that got you through your past will get you through your present.

You have been through some stuff. You have faced giants in your life. You have been knocked down a time or two. But you're still here! And that same grace that got you to this point will get you to your new future. There is hope, because we serve a God full of grace!

I encourage you to put Hebrews 4:16 to practice right now:

> *Let us then with confidence draw near to the throne of grace, that we may receive mercy and find grace to help in time of need. —Hebrews 4:16 (ESV)*

Take a moment out of each day to enter God's throne room. You have access to it by faith in Jesus! You can be a total mess and still enter. Get down on your knees, close your eyes, and pray boldly to the God of grace. Ask Him for more. Ask Him to multiply the grace on you so that you can walk through your trial with peace and confidence. Then watch Him do it. He is faithful. God wants to give good gifts to His children, and one of the greatest gifts He offers is the grace that empowers us to rise above every storm and press on to victory!

SCRIPTURE STUDY:

ISAIAH 26:3
You keep him in perfect peace whose mind is stayed on you, because he trusts in you.

PHILIPPIANS 4:13
I can do all things through him who strengthens me.

JOURNAL THOUGHTS:

Take a moment to write a prayer to God. Imagine you are entering His throne room with your words, and gaining access to His unlimited grace for your situation.

_____

_____

_____

_____

_____

_____

_____

_____

_____

_____

_____

_____

_____

_____

_____

_____

MISSION IMPOSSIBLE

CHAPTER 2

*But Jesus looked at them and said, "With man
this is impossible, but with God all things are
possible."—Matthew 19:26 (ESV)*

D o you feel like you've reached your limit? Do you find yourself telling those closest to you that you're going to explode if one more thing goes wrong? Do you dream of running away to a far-off land where nobody needs you, everyone is happy, and the sun always shines? My friend, I have good news. You are not alone, and there's a grace for that.

God's grace is available for those moments when we have reached our natural limits. In fact, God wants you to get to the place where you rely on that grace to get through. Even the strongest of biblical heroes reached their limit at one point or another.

*But he said to me, "My grace is sufficient
for you, for my power is made perfect in
weakness."—2 Corinthians 12:9*

When the apostle Paul was sick and tired of dealing with the thorn in his side, he pleaded for God to remove it. He begged God three times to take it from him. We don't know exactly what the thorn was. Maybe he was dealing with a real physical pain. Maybe it was a relational pain, a person he was stuck with, who was causing him trouble. Maybe he was dealing with a circumstance that required a miracle. Regardless, for this incredibly strong man to plead for God to remove it, it must have been terrible. I don't know what your thorn is, but I know mine. I know that trouble that I wish God would just remove from my life. In fact, if you're like me, you can probably name a couple of thorns. We can spend our time worrying about that thing, complaining about it, and stressing about it, or we can receive the grace that God offers to deal with it. God didn't promise to remove the thorn for Paul, but He promised that His supernatural grace would be sufficient to handle it. And the same is true for you and me. We would love for God to "poof" our worries away, change that person, or provide that miracle. **We want God to work on our circumstances, but oftentimes, God uses our circumstances to work on us.** God may not change your surroundings, but He will absolutely give you the grace to handle those things.

HOT TUB REVELATIONS

It was a typical week for me, and by typical, I mean I was trying to do more than I was capable of realistically doing. The only thing that got me through was knowing we had a little getaway planned for the family that weekend. I had booked a night at a themed hotel, with a pool and a hot tub, as a celebration for the largest book sale I had received since publishing my first book. (I make it a priority to let the kids experience the rewards of ministry, since they automatically get a front-row seat to the sacrifices of ministry.) I booked the biggest room they had, the Pirate Ship Suite. For two days, Justin and I left the ministry world behind to get some quality time with the kids. While they splashed in the pool, Justin and I took turns getting some alone time in the hot tub. As I sat in the glorious solitude of the bubbling spa, I closed my eyes and had a moment with God. I wanted family time, but I also knew I was running low on mental capacity. I needed an extra dose of grace. Alone in the hot tub, I literally prayed, "Okay God, we've got ten minutes. Talk to me." And He did. He inspired me to stretch. Literally, stand up in the water, and stretch my body out. I blindly obeyed. Thankfully, nobody was watching as I did yoga poses alone in the hot tub. While stretching, I learned a great lesson from my Creator. He said this: "When you reach your limit, it's called a stretch." I was reminded of all the times that week I must have said, "I'm going to lose it! I'm going to run away! Mommy is going to explode!" But I wasn't going to explode. I wasn't losing it. I was actually being stretched. I was reaching my natural limits, and that's right where God comes in, if I let Him. I made a decision to change my perspective on limits. No longer would I let my natural limits be the end of me. I was determined to use those moments as opportunities to press into the limitless strength of my Heavenly Father, knowing He uses those moments to prepare me for more.

Every season stretches us for the next. If we do not allow ourselves to be stretched, we will not increase our capacity. If we don't increase our capacity, we won't be prepared for the next level God wants to take us to.

Do you feel yourself being stretched? Does it hurt a little bit? Does it make you scream sometimes? Does it make you want to turn back? Every great athlete knows the importance of stretching before an event. God is preparing you for the next event, the next promotion, the next blessing, the next season of life, and if you want to be able to receive it, you must choose not to turn back but to press into that stretch, and let God work through you.

That night in the hot tub, God met me right where I was, and He refreshed my soul. He changed my perspective and filled my spiritual cup. I had no clue what was about to happen, but He sure did, and boy am I glad, looking back, that I had that moment before what came next.

On the way out of the pool that night, we passed by the receptionist desk in the lobby, where a woman named Trish stood, looking a little down. I had spoken with her briefly as we checked in and later when we ordered dinner. I couldn't help but notice how lonely she looked behind the desk.

Maybe it was just my overly empathetic personality, or maybe it was a divine nudge. I took the kids back to the hotel room, grabbed one of my books and set back out to the lobby to talk with Trish. I wasn't sure how to approach her or if she'd even be up for a conversation, but I took a risk and began with a simple question: "Do you like to read?" That question birthed a friendship. I told her about my journey of authoring, and she told me her testimony. I was blown away as she told me how God given her the strength to overcome an addiction to heroin. She spoke about life in addiction and her new life afterward. She smiled as she talked about how grateful she was just to have a job, a home, and her own car. She praised God for a second chance at life, and she told me of her passion to help other addicts find freedom. She said, "Sometimes I'll see a girl on the street and know exactly what she's dealing with, because I've been there. So I'll stop and tell her my story, in hopes of helping her overcome." I handed her a copy of *Finding Strength* and encouraged her to keep telling her testimony every chance she got. Later that night, we connected on social media, and she told me how grateful she was that God would bring our paths together that night. I had no intentions of doing ministry on that family trip, but when God fills your soul with His grace, you can't help but to reach out to someone else!

YOUR MISSION IMPOSSIBLE

I don't know what mission you have been assigned in this life, but I know that there will be times when it seems impossible to finish it. I know there will be times when you are confused about which path to take. I know there will be times when you want to quit. That's why I have written this book, Grace for the Race. So that you can find the grace needed to keep running your race, and to finish it strong.

EPHESIANS 2:10
For we are his workmanship, created in Christ Jesus for good works, which God prepared beforehand, that we should walk in them.

In what area of your life do you feel you're being stretched? This is not the end of you—this is preparation for what's next. What purpose could lie ahead for you in this very area?

_____

_____

_____

_____

_____

_____

_____

_____

_____

_____

_____

_____

_____

_____

_____

_____

_____

_____

BY GRACE, THROUGH FAITH

CHAPTER 3

Now to Him who is able to do exceedingly
abundantly above all that we ask or think,
according to the power that works in us, [21] *to*
Him be glory in the church by Christ Jesus to
all generations, forever and ever. Amen.
—Ephesians 3:20–21

D o you have big dreams? Do you fantasize about a different life, and the things you would do if only you were brave enough to risk it all to pursue them? What is it that holds you back from living that life? Is it a job? Children? Family responsibilities? Bills? Or maybe it's none of those things. Maybe it's comfort that keeps you from fulfilling your God-given dreams.

THE COST OF COMFORT

When my son, Kaden, was about three years old, he came to me, exhausted and panting, with a big bag of oranges in his hand. He politely

asked me to open the bag so he could have one. Like any good mom, I agreed, impressed that he carried the heavy bag all the way through the house to find me. But what happened next created a teaching point that I use to this day, even with adults. I asked him to put the bag of oranges back in the kitchen, to which he replied, "I can't. It's too heavy."
It wasn't too heavy a moment ago, but now that he had what he wanted, the motivation to carry the bag was gone.

Many of us get to that place in life, where **we finally get what we were fighting for, and we lose motivation to continue doing the hard things that got us there.** Think about marriage. When you were dating, you wrote little love notes. He opened the door and bought flowers. She told him how good-lookin' he was and cooked fancy meals. But after that wedding band is placed, something happens. We lose motivation to continue doing what is good and right, to keep our marriage passionate and intimate. When I counsel married couples, my goal is not to fix their problems. My goal is to get them to fall in love again. If I can get them doing the things they did at first, their problems will take care of themselves.

> *But I have this complaint against you. You*
> *don't love me or each other as you did at first!*
> *⁵Look how far you have fallen! Turn back to*
> *me and do the works you did at first.*
> *—Revelation 2:4–5 (NLT)*

Marriage isn't the only place this happens. What about your education? When you have a goal, such as a degree or a certification in mind, you study hard, you stay up late, you put in the work to get that next piece of paper that says you're important, but are you willing to continue working on yourself, to read, study, and apply new learning to make yourself a better version of you, even when there is no reward in sight?

How does this apply to your work life? When you're going after that big promotion, you show up early, stay late, work hard, put away the distractions, and give your best. But are you willing to do all those things when you don't have a carrot dangling in front of you?

> *"Nothing so conclusively proves a man's ability*
> *to lead others, as what he does from day to day*
> *to lead himself." —Thomas J. Watson*

Now when it comes to our dreams and goals, could it be comfort keeping you from pursuing what God has asked of you? Does it scare you to think of sacrificing everything that is comfortable and convenient for an unknown future? What if you fail, and everyone talks about it? What if nobody believes in you, and you turn out a fool? These are all thoughts that men and women who have achieved great things had before they stepped out in faith.

Imagine Noah, responding to God's command to build an ark when it had never rained. Imagine Abraham leaving his hometown and all he had ever known to wander into the unknown with his wife and family. Imagine Elisha telling his family that he is done working for a living and he is going into the miracle business. Imagine Paul leaving his position of leadership within the Jewish religion to become a traitor, only to be met with opposition, beatings, and imprisonment.

Are you willing to abandon comfort to pursue God's call on your life?

ABANDON COZY

Every January Justin and I, along with our entire leadership team, spend twenty-one days in prayer and fasting, seeking God for a word for the year. This past year, Justin and I got away for the day to a cabin in the middle of nowhere, to pray and rest during our fast. There was zero cell phone service, so we were completely free from distraction. This cabin sits on eighty-five acres of beautiful forest. That afternoon, Justin decided to go for a hike and invited me to go along with him. I had a tough decision to make: bundle up and spend the next forty-five minutes hiking uphill in zero-degree temperatures, or stay by the fire and take a nap. I bid farewell to my overzealous hubby and cuddled up on the couch with a warm blanket. When he came back in, he told me of the beautiful scenery. He had hiked up the side of the hill twice and snowboarded down. As he described the peaceful snow-covered forest and the fantastic view from the top, I began to get a little envious. Then he hit me where it hurts. He said, "As soon as I got to the top, I could see deer running, and I was so far up that I could watch them run across the whole side of the hill." He knows how much I love to watch animals in nature. As I lay there in my cozy blanket, I began to toss around the idea of going out on my own. From the inside of that cabin, the snowy terrain looked tempting, but I was just so comfortable.

This is where many of us get stuck when it comes to our decisions in life. We want to pursue that dream, but how can we possibly change careers now? We want to do more in ministry, but that would require a shift change, or a pay cut, and life is too comfortable to make that kind of sacrifice. But I wonder: What is on the other side of your decision to leave comfort and step out in faith? The devil doesn't always hit us with difficult things; sometimes he gets us off course with just the opposite. **The devil doesn't always throw darts. Sometimes he throws blankets.**

As I looked at the clock, I determined that I would have to leave that instant to make it all the way up the hill and back down before we had to leave for home. I threw off the blanket and began to prepare for the frigid temperatures.

This is the first step. Throw off the blanket. Decide today that comfort is not the goal. **Remind yourself that what you want *most* is more important than what you want *now*.** Begin to prepare for what God wants to do through you in this next season. Don't wait for Him to make the first move—you start doing the work, through faith, and watch Him come alongside you!

Justin encouraged me to dress warmly, but all I had were some leggings and a pair of sweatpants for my lower half, so he grabbed

some large Carhartt bibs from the closet and helped me into them.
I looked like young David trying on King Saul's armor before facing
Goliath. There was no way I could even walk in them, let alone hike
up a mountain. I threw off the bibs, threw on as many layers as I
could, and set out to find some deer.

I only made it about twenty feet up the incline before I began to
breathe heavy. I realized quickly this was not going to be a walk in the
park. The goal was to get to the top of this hill, where I would find a
tree stand to climb, and then look over the whole valley, but it was a
steep hike the whole way. About halfway there I started to wonder if I
could make it. About two-thirds of the way, I began to sing the lyrics
from the Lauren Daigle song, "Lord let this be…where I die." I was
exhausted. My heart was beating out of my chest. My legs were jello.
I looked up and caught sight of the tree stand. It looked so far away,
and I was already out of breath. I looked to my left, and I could see
the valley, the rolling hills, and the sun shining down. **I thought for a
moment, "This is good enough."**

And that, my friend, is where many more dreamers get stuck: "good
enough." You begin the work God asked of you. You realize once you're
in it, that it's much harder than you expected, but you've seen some of the
good fruit that came from it, and you start to settle in. You tell yourself
things like, "God doesn't need me to do anything great. He has other
people who can fill those shoes. I have done some good, and I am content
with living right here." But, my friend, **there is more**, if you will press on.

After a couple minutes' break, I looked back up at the tree stand and
began stepping again. With every pant of breath I began to grunt
a little, determined to make it to the top. I am not one to give up,
even if nobody is watching, and even if it means nothing in the
end. I would rather make it there and find out it wasn't worth it,
than to stay at the bottom of the hill wondering. As the tree stand
became clearer, I realized I had seen wrong before. It wasn't as far as
I'd thought. I praised God for moving the tree stand! With a final
grunt and a push of my hiking sticks, I made it to the top and looked

out onto a glorious winter wonderland. Hills and valleys, trees and homes, all sparkling in the afternoon sun. I climbed the tree stand and sat at the top for a while, admiring God's creation. It was then He spoke to me. He said, "This is how I see your life. Not in chronological order, like you see it. I see it as one big picture, full of hills and valleys, but they all come together to make something beautiful."

That day I left my comfort zone to go find some deer. In the end, I didn't spot one animal, but I received something much greater: a moment with my Heavenly Father.

When you decide to leave comfort behind and pursue what God is calling you to do, you may think you know what you're shooting for. You may even have a big five-year plan for God to bless. But God will give you exceedingly, abundantly above all that you could ask, think, or imagine. It will be harder than you expected. You will be tempted to quit. You will be tempted to settle for less than God's best. But don't stop until you reach the fulfilled, abundant, grace-filled, fruitful life that He has called you to. You may not get what you wanted, but you will get so much more.

THERE IS MORE

I want you to imagine your dream...and then think MORE. I don't necessarily mean more money or more fame—those things aren't always the goal. I mean more of God's goodness in your life. I mean more fulfillment when you lay your head down at night. I mean more of God's grace and gifts overflowing through you and around you.

I happen to believe that God wants more for you than you want for yourself. He would love nothing more than to see you prosper spiritually, physically, financially, and in every area of life. When Jesus walked the earth, He told us why He came:

> *I have come that they may have life, and that they*
> *may have it more abundantly.—John 10:10*

God doesn't want to harm you. He doesn't like to see you hurt. He didn't sacrifice His life for you so that you could simply endure a nine-to-five job long enough to retire comfortably. In fact, comfort isn't even the goal! God has plans for you that are higher, greater, and more abundant than you can imagine, but pursuing them is going to require FAITH! He wants to use you in ways that seem impossible. He has planted desires, gifts, passions, and abilities within you, not for them to lay dormant for thirty years, but for you to use them, by grace, through faith.

I wonder how different this world would look if we all stopped living as our society says is "normal" and we started every day, every season, and every year of our life surrendering to God and asking Him what He wants us to do, and then acting on it. I bet we would see more people smiling, more couples holding hands in public, more confident children, and more joy-filled homes, because there is nothing more fulfilling than living the life God has called you to. That doesn't mean it is easy, but it is definitely worth it. I don't think the problem is a lack of dreams, or a lack of dreamers. I believe the problem is a lack of faith, and faith is the only way to achieve anything worthwhile!

SCRIPTURE STUDY:

HEBREWS 11:6 (NIV)
And without faith it is impossible to please God, because anyone who comes to him must believe that he exists and that he rewards those who earnestly seek him.

EPHESIANS 2:8 (ESV)
For by grace you have been saved through faith.

JOURNAL PROMPTS:

Read the story of Elisha in 1 Kings 19 and take notes. (Elisha burned the plows in order to follow God's call on his life. His plows were his livelihood, so in burning them, he removed any chance of Plan B and pursued the life of a prophet by faith.)

What source of comfort and security must you sacrifice in order to step out in faith?

HOT MESS EXPRESS

CHAPTER 4

She is clothed with strength and dignity;
she can laugh at the days to come.
—Proverbs 31:25 (NIV)

I want so badly to be the Proverbs 31 woman. Every now and then I see glimpses of her in me. I wake up early, pour the coffee, open my Bible, and pray to the Father before I begin my day. Ah, the peace of obedience and communion with the Almighty. It feels good. I feel good. I feel like a swan gliding gracefully into her day. Surely nothing can take my peace today. Then someone hits this swan with an oar, water splashes all over my beautiful feathers, and I fly off the handle! I turn from graceful swan into raging dragon in moments, and those closest to me end up getting burned.

I wish I could stay in a place of peace and serenity with God all day and never accept a ticket to ride on the hot mess express. I want to appear poised and respond perfectly to all situations in life, but all too often, I allow my mind and emotions to veer off of the straight and narrow and into the weeds.

Do you relate? Do you find yourself responding emotionally or irrationally to little problems? Do you let your temper have its way and make you say things you know you don't mean? Do you let people stress you out to the point that you want to run away and never come back? Do you take on too many responsibilities and end up hating life when they all pile up at once? Welcome to the hot mess express. Let's go for a quick ride together and then find our way off, shall we?

HEROES IN DISTRESS

We are not alone, friends. In fact, these feelings and issues we have are age-old problems that even the most noble of Bible heroes experienced in their time. King David, who wrote many Psalms, has been such a comfort to me when I find myself losing it. Within the Psalms, we read time and time again when David was so distressed that he complained, pleaded, and even questioned God. His prayers were real, honest, and raw. He sang songs of praise, but he also sang songs of pain. One of my favorites to read when I'm frustrated is Psalm 13.

> *How long, O LORD? Will you forget me forever?*
> *How long will you hide your face from me?*
> *² How long must I take counsel in my soul and*
> *have sorrow in my heart all the day?*
> *How long shall my enemy be exalted over me?*
> *³ Consider and answer me, O LORD my God;*
> *light up my eyes, lest I sleep the sleep of death,*
> *⁴ lest my enemy say, "I have prevailed over him,"*
> *lest my foes rejoice because I am shaken.*
> *⁵ But I have trusted in your steadfast love; my heart*
> *shall rejoice in your salvation.*
> *⁶ I will sing to the LORD, because he has dealt*
> *bountifully with me.*
> *—Psalm 13 (ESV)*

In the beginning of this psalm, David feels forgotten, threatened, and full of sorrow. He is in anguish. He asks questions that many of us find ourselves asking when we're frustrated. He wonders if he is going to die in his sorrow. And he doesn't withhold these feelings from his Holy God. He lays it all out there, unfiltered. I wonder how often we get honest with God about how we're feeling. I wonder if he is waiting for us to come to Him with an authentic prayer, pursuing His presence in our deepest despair, and asking for help. I once heard a pastor say, "The most honest and powerful prayer you can pray is one word long…'help.'"

When the bills are piling up, when the diagnosis is frightening, when family is letting you down, when schedules are crazy, when the pressure is rising, do you take your needs to the One who can handle it all? Do you get real, raw, and honest with your Creator, admitting your need for Him? I think if we did, we would find that He desires those types of conversations.

Imagine your son or daughter around age three. They want a cup of milk. They climb the counter to reach the cups and bang their head on the cabinet door. They knock down all the dishes in their attempt to find their perfect cup. They make it off the counter, but not without bumping their knee in the process. They get to the fridge, only to find that they can't reach the milk. You're watching all this go down, and you notice the frustration on their little face as they meet struggle after struggle. Finally, they fall to the floor, flailing their legs and crying that they're never going to get their milk. If you are like me, you watch peacefully from the other side of the kitchen and wait for them to ask for help. Then you say something like, "All you had to do was come to me and ask for help, and I would have gotten you some milk."

Your Heavenly Father is not bothered by your requests. He wants to help you. He has time for you. He has energy for you. He has help for you!

> *Let us then with confidence draw near to the*
> *throne of grace, that we may receive mercy and*

find grace to help in time of need.—Hebrews
4:16 (ESV)

God is watching you. Not to judge you. Not to punish you. To help you. He wants you to turn around, tell Him about your day, and ask for help. He is ready and willing to open doors, provide for your needs, and rebuke your enemies. Will you be like David and get honest with God, rather than fly off the handle with your family? If we can do this, I believe we will experience a transition in the midst of our prayers, just as David did in this psalm:

> *But I have trusted in your steadfast love;*
> *my heart shall rejoice in your salvation.*
> *⁶ I will sing to the LORD,*
> *because he has dealt bountifully with me.*
> *—Psalm 13:5–6*

Once David brought his frustrations and honest concerns to God, he was reminded of God's faithfulness. **His mind transitioned from pain to praise.** His heart transformed from agony to joy. His problems no longer looked impossible. He no longer felt alone. His worries were silenced in the presence of his Father. He did just what Hebrews 4:16 says. He approached the throne with boldness and received mercy and help in his time of need.

If you start your day a graceful swan gliding through life, but you end it looking more like a spazzed cat fighting bath time, don't fret. God gets you. David was a human, with real human struggles and emotions, and God understood that. He understands you too. He knows you are going to fail now and then. He knows you are going to lose your cool. He knows how you will respond when things don't go as planned. **He knows what gets under your skin. And guess what? He has plenty of grace to cover that.** So, don't feel ashamed when you find yourself a hot mess. Bring it to God, and let Him replace your sorrow with serenity.

A PRINCESS STORY

Jennifer Beckham, author of *Get Over Yourself*, writes about her journey to a lifelong dream of becoming a Disney Princess and the harsh realization that it wasn't all sunshine and rainbows. Jennifer found herself struggling with bulimia and depression, far from home, and forced to put on a princess smile for the world. After unloading her emotions to her boss one day, in hopes of being sent home, she was hit with these harsh words:

> "Who ever told you to feel? You were chosen to be a princess. Now go, wash your face, get a new attitude, put on your clothes, and go be Cinderella!" (*Get Over Yourself*, Jennifer Beckham, pg. 24)

Jennifer spends the rest of the book helping readers get over their pasts, their emotions, their issues, and get on with their God-given purpose!

We all experience moments when our emotions get the best of us. Moments when the pressures of life and frustrations of unmet expectations lead us straight to the hot mess express. The good news is, we don't have to live in bondage to our emotions!

STOP PLAYING SIMON SAYS

Do you remember the childhood game, Simon Says? Whenever the leader gives a command and prefaces it with "Simon says," you must do the command. Oftentimes, we allow our emotions to take the role of Simon and tell us what to do.

- A family member calls with bad news, and you respond emotionally, before ever consulting with God.

- The drama queen at work pulls you aside before your shift and tells you all the reasons you should be upset with so-and-so. Before you've even clocked in, you're fed up with your workplace and ready to quit.

- Your child ignores your very clear instructions not to run around the coffee table with a bowl of cereal and dumps mushy Lucky Charms all over your rug. You're prepared to sell a child on behalf of a $200 piece of furniture.

- Your spouse comes home in a bad mood, ranting and raving about their day, without taking a moment to ask how yours was, and you're tempted to top their complaints with a few complaints of your own. How dare they think their day was anything compared to yours?

If we ever want to get off of the hot mess express, we have got to stop playing Simon Says with our emotions. Just because someone else gets dramatic and emotional toward us does not mean we need to respond emotionally. We can actually take a moment to ourselves, say a small prayer, take a deep breath, and proceed with God's grace.

A few years back Justin and I got into one of those fights that usually ends with someone throwing something or leaving the house. I can't even remember what we were fighting about, but I'm sure it wasn't as important as it seemed at the time. At one point, I stomped out of the house, sure that I wasn't returning until he apologized and confessed that I was right. But a few steps out into my garage, I felt the Holy Spirit nudging me to listen to his perspective. I stopped in my tracks, took a deep breath, and said, "What?!" I really didn't want to hear what God had to say at this point, because I had no intentions of obeying. But that moment with God changed something on the inside of me that I can hardly put into words. I put my emotions on the backburner and decided to turn around. I walked back into the house, straight up to Justin, and said, "Somewhere deep down inside, I love you." And against everything within me, I gave him a hug. I can't tell you how difficult it was, but I'm glad I did it.

I wish I could tell you that I respond that way every time we get in an argument, but I don't. Sometimes my emotions win. Sometimes I accept the ticket to the hot mess express. But as I grow closer to God, those moments are fewer and further between. We don't have to live in bondage to our emotions, friend. We don't have to play Simon Says. We can choose to take a break, go to God, and respond with grace-filled words and actions.

LAST STOP

So, how do we get off the hot mess express? Take it to God. All of it. When people make you want to move to a faraway land and never return, take it to God. When your schedule makes you want to crawl into a hole and hide, take it to God. When bills are piling as high as your laundry, take it to God. When your spouse makes you want to scream, take it to God. When your kids have swiped your last nerve and taken it for a ride, take it to God. Take it all to Him. He already knows what you need. He watched you bonk your head on the cabinet door, bump your knee on the counter, and fall to the floor in frustration. He is standing there, strong and peaceful, ready to help.

GALATIANS 5:1 (ESV)
For freedom Christ has set us free; stand firm therefore, and do not submit again to a yoke of slavery.

PHILIPPIANS 4:8 (ESV)
Finally, brothers, whatever is true, whatever is honorable, whatever is just, whatever is pure, whatever is lovely, whatever is commendable, if there is any excellence, if there is anything worthy of praise, think about these things.

GALATIANS 5:22–23 (ESV)
But the fruit of the Spirit is love, joy, peace, patience, kindness, goodness, faithfulness, gentleness, self-control; against such things there is no law.

JOURNAL THOUGHTS:

How do you usually respond when things don't go your way?

What emotion tends to get the best of you?

What can you do to stop responding emotionally and start responding gracefully?

_____

_____

_____

_____

_____

_____

_____

_____

REST BETWEEN BATTLES

CHAPTER 5

*Come to me, all who labor and are heavy
laden, and I will give you rest.*
—Matthew 11:28 (ESV)

Do you ever think back to your childhood and wish you would have enjoyed it more? Do you wish you could tell your eight-year-old self to have more fun, make more mud pies, swing a little higher, and play a little longer? I do. I wish I could tell young Mindy to stop trying to grow up and enjoy being little.

In the same way, in this very season, although there are plenty of things vying for your attention, God is calling you to enjoy it. He wishes you could see from His perspective, from an eternal perspective. He wishes you wouldn't worry so much, try so hard to be different, or wish away the season you're in. You will only be this age once. Your life will only look this way for a season. Your family will change. Your circumstances will change. So why not take some time to enjoy this day?

It wasn't too long ago a mentor of mine, Pastor Brooke Butcher, gave me some incredible advice. She said, "Rest between the battles." At that point, rest was not something I was good at. I have always been future-focused, eyes set on the next big thing I want to do for God. But I realize that this is not a strength but a weakness, because my constant desire for what is to come distracts me from what is here now. I have a hard time resting because I feel guilty for not doing more. I have a hard time enjoying my life when I know there is someone else out there who is hurting. I have a tendency to use every ounce of my energy and time being productive, rather than enjoying my life. But once I heard this advice, I began to put it into practice. I realized that I was in a season that had minimal battles. Sure, every day seemed like a battle as a mom of four small kids and pastor of a growing church, but when I really looked at my life as a whole, there weren't any major catastrophes that required my attention. So I decided to relax a little. I stopped pushing myself so hard to reach the next goal. Then, when tragedy struck, I had the capacity to help.

If we don't rest between battles, we will experience compassion fatigue. Many parents, teachers, servicemen and women, and healthcare workers experience this. **Compassion fatigue happens when we focus on caring for others without practicing self-care.** We end up spending all of our emotional, mental, and physical capacity, leaving us feeling tired, bitter, and even apathetic if it goes on too long. This is why resting between battles is vital.

When I think back to my first few years of parenting, I remember being stressed out, tired, and mentally drained. Ten years later, I have a totally different perspective on motherhood. Oh, how I wish I could go back and redo some of those years. I would give nearly anything to squeeze their little cheeks or hear their toddler voices again. Now their diapers, bottles, and toys have been replaced with jerseys, cleats, leotards, and devices. But this year, we go back to the baby phase, as baby Ross number five joins us this summer! I am excited to revisit this phase again, but this time with a different perspective (and some helpers)!

We can't allow the pressure of the future or the regrets of our past distract us from the here and now. So what can we do? **If your future self could**

give you advice for today, what would it be? I bet it would sound something like this: enjoy this season. I know it's hard, but it's not as bad as it seems. There are beautiful moments amidst the messy ones. There are memories being made that you will cherish forever. Those things that you think are important are not as important as you think. Rest more. You need it. Take care of yourself. Do the things you enjoy. Stress less. Look your kids in the eye. Let them run in and out and get your floors a mess. They only get to play for so long. Smile at your spouse. Tell them you love them. Don't push away when they hug you. Stop rushing so much. Make time for the important things. Laugh. Walk in the sunshine. And rest between the battles.

WALLS OF JERICHO

Life is full of battles, but between them are opportunities for rest, relaxation, and enjoyment. Sometimes right in the middle of a battle, God will give us moments of rest and joy. Joshua was a mighty man of God, given the charge to lead God's people into the Promised Land. At one point, God gave him the instructions to lead an army around the walls of Jericho, marching silently every day for seven days. Each day they were to march around the city walls one time, and seven times on the last day. You may be familiar with the story. What many people miss about this story is that God's people had to rest between the marches. Before the mission was over, while the enemy was still on the other side of that wall, they were forced to rest, trusting that God would come through on the seventh day.

Maybe you find yourself in the battle right now and you are having a hard time resting, because there is more to be done. You feel guilty taking a nap. You feel guilty taking a break. Those thoughts are not from God. Rest is a commandment from the One who created you, and it is one of the most powerful statements you can make toward the enemy. **When we rest amidst the battle, we are showing our faith and trust in God.** We are proving that we believe He fights for us, even as we sleep.

On the seventh day, those walls came crashing down by the power of

God. The Israelites could not have made those walls come down any earlier. They could have wasted time complaining, worrying, striving, and praying, but the walls had an appointed demo day and nothing they did could have moved it up. So why worry, friend? Why waste sleep over that battle you're facing? Why toil and tarry over things that you can't control? **God has an appointed demolition day for your battle to be over.** Trust His plan. Get rest. And believe that He is working on your behalf!

SCRIPTURE STUDY:

EXODUS 20:8–10 (NIV)
Remember the Sabbath day by keeping it holy. Six days you shall labor and do all your work, but the seventh day is a sabbath to the LORD your God. On it you shall not do any work, neither you, nor your son or daughter, nor your male or female servant, nor your animals, nor any foreigner residing in your towns.

PSALM 4:8 (ESV)
In peace I will both lie down and sleep; for you alone, O Lord, make me dwell in safety.

JOURNAL PROMPTS:

Am I in the middle of a battle right now or between battles?

How can I practice resting in this season?

Write down those burdens that you are carrying right now, or that battle that you need God to win, and hand it over to Him. Choose to do the most brave, powerful thing you can do to prove your faith in God: rest.

_____

_____

_____

_____

_____

_____

_____

_____

_____

REST AMIDST THE CHAOS

CHAPTER 6

The Lord is my shepherd; I shall not want.
² He makes me lie down in green pastures.
He leads me beside still waters.
³ He restores my soul.
—Psalm 23:1–3 (ESV)

In all my conversations with fellow leaders and ministry volunteers, one theme is evident: they don't like to rest. Their beautiful hearts for God and servant tendencies make a huge impact on a weekly basis in the church and community, but if they aren't careful, they will join the ranks of former soldiers who burnt out. The last thing I want for my leaders is to see them fall into this trap of high-pressure, never-resting schedules that lead straight to breakdown. So, every chance we get, we do check-ups. I ask them when the last time was that they took a Sabbath day of rest, when their last date with their spouse was, and when their next vacation with their family is scheduled. It is vital to me that I raise up leaders who are well-balanced, well-rested, and healthy. In order to do that, I must go first. So, below are a couple non-negotiables in my life that help me stay balanced. I hope they can help you create your own!

DATE NIGHT

"Hey look! It's Al Pacino!" Justin exclaimed as the hot coffee spit out of my mouth and nose at the same time. From the second floor of the mall, he and I shared a coffee and people-watched for over an hour, making up names for random strangers, talking in accents, and finding look-alikes for all our favorite celebrities. We were in a season when expensive dinners (or even cheap dinners) were not an option for date night, but we could afford a cup of coffee and some chocolate to share for dessert. We had four kids, mountains of debt, and bills that only got paid when the collectors called, but date night was not negotiable. Every week we got a few hours to just be husband and wife. In that time we were able to talk about things we never had time to discuss during the week, dream together about our future goals, laugh (a lot), and look each other in the eye with smiles, rather than disdain. If you are a married person, these moments are critical to the longevity and health of your marriage. You must have time together when you aren't working, planning, caring for children, or giving status updates. Time to simply be husband and wife. Over the years, it has gotten easier to make time and money for date nights as our schedules eased up and income increased. But it wasn't always easy. There were seasons when we were both working two jobs, trying to make rent and take care of babies, but we still made time for dates. Sometimes those dates were midnight dates, after the kids had gone to bed (those were some of the best ones). Sometimes date night meant asking a friend to babysit for free and playing Pictionary at the coffee shop. **We had to get creative, and if you are going to have a marriage that lasts beyond the statistics, you will have to get creative too.** If all this sounds impossible with your schedule and budget, start where you can. Maybe for now you can do once a month. Maybe you can try for every other week. Maybe it will require a shift change or a firm conversation with your boss about your hours. Even if that is the case, I guarantee you won't regret putting your marriage first above your job, because God honors when we prioritize our schedule to be in line with His word. As you make the tough decisions to put your spouse first, you may experience initial pushback, because the enemy of our souls hates marriage and everything it symbolizes. He will do his best to steal, kill, and destroy your marriage. But God is working on your behalf, and as you do things His way, He will open doors, provide resources, and pour out blessings on you.

SABBATH REST

So God blessed the seventh day and made it
holy, because on it God rested from all his work
that he had done in creation.
—Genesis 2:3 (ESV)

Even God Almighty, Creator of the Universe, allowed Himself to rest from His work. Who are we to think that we don't need rest? Our bodies were made in His image and created for six days of work and one day of rest. Sadly today, the Sabbath is rarely honored and taken as a day of rest. Many families spend their weekdays in school and work and their weekends running around doing sports, events, parties, and overtime. If this describes your life, don't feel bad. That's not the goal of this chapter. Guilt won't get you any closer to experiencing God's grace in your life. Even great leaders in ministry have a hard time making rest a priority, because what they do never seems to end. Pastors carry their congregation with them everywhere from the office to the bedroom, on that little evil device that allows people to invade their life in any and every waking moment, and sometimes even sleeping moments! As a whole, we have abandoned the Sabbath, and all its benefits, for the sake of all things urgent. **But what if the urgent is leading you away from the important?** When you look back at your life in twenty years, will you be able to confidently say you enjoyed your life, or will it have been such a blur of busyness that you barely remember it? I can only speak for myself, but I want to look back on this season and know that I appreciated it while it was here. I want to slow down enough to not just smell the roses, but to appreciate my daughter's giggle, listen to my son's stories, and ask my husband how his day was. I can't be that person if I don't get rest.

THE BEAST

Let me be honest. When I don't rest, I am a force to be reckoned with, and not in a good way. I throw fits, stomp my feet, raise my voice, throw my phone, and pout like a baby. I allow my temper to get the best of me, and then allow pity to throw me a party. When I push myself beyond my healthy limits, I begin to dream of running away. I imagine everyone in my life wishing I would return as they notice piles of laundry mounding up around them, the cat losing weight because nobody fed her, recitals and assignments missed because no one kept a calendar, and the electricity shut off because nobody paid the bill. When I begin to feel like I do everything, and nobody appreciates it, I know it's time for rest. Nowadays, these moments of unleashing the beast are fewer and farther between, because I have gained control of my calendar and held myself responsible for planning my rest. I also allow myself a day to "catch up," which relieves a lot of the pressure that builds up throughout the week. My catch-up day comes before my day of rest, because otherwise I would be a stressed-out mess thinking about everything I have to do. Mondays are usually catch-up days. After a strong cup of coffee, I make my giant to-do list, throw on some yoga pants, and conquer the universe. I usually get about two-thirds of the way down the list before the day ends, but I feel much better than I did in the morning.

Fridays are my Sabbath. Keep in mind, a Sabbath day of rest does not have to be on Sunday. For Justin and me, Sundays are work days. We wake up at 4:30 a.m., pray, rehearse, lead teams, run multiple services, minister until we've got nothing left, and go home exhausted. So we make Fridays our Sabbath. What do we do on Sabbath? It's not all napping, praying, and reading our Bibles, although those things are definitely included! Sometimes we go for a hike or drive through the country, admiring the scenery. Sometimes we catch a movie. Sometimes we go on a date and take advantage of combining two of our priorities into one day. In fact, the day of rest makes for a great day for a date, because you've spent some time unwinding before you come together. Conversations are lighter, happier, and more intimate when we're rested.

Just yesterday was my day of rest this week. I can tell you there were plenty of things to do, and plenty of people who wanted my attention, but I put it all aside. I know oftentimes, what is urgent is not always what is important. Toward the end of the day, I was starting to feel the itch to get some ministry work done. I was tempted to pull out my laptop and crank out a few tasks while no one was looking. Justin was out of the house and the kids were all in their rooms playing well. As I walked over to my laptop, I stopped myself. I reminded myself that God would help me accomplish everything I needed during the rest of the week if I would keep the Sabbath, like I planned. So instead, I picked up a great book, sat back down on the couch, and enjoyed some quiet time with one of my heroes in the faith, Joyce Meyer. In her book *Eat the Cookie, Buy the Shoes*, Joyce talks about the importance of rest and enjoyment. As I read her stories, I laughed, I related, and I felt tremendously refreshed. I was thankful for that time, because little did I know, I would need that rest and refreshment to be my best self the next morning.

Mornings are pretty crazy around here with four school-age kiddos. They all take the same bus, which means they all wake up at the same time, fight over bathrooms and clothes, and yell for my help every five minutes. I usually end up pushing them out the door as the bus rounds the corner. This morning, amidst the busyness, I made a silly decision to check my emails. I noticed that around 3:00 a.m. I had received an email titled, "Thank you for your purchase." I opened it to find that my seven-year-old daughter had spent $107.00 on video games during the night. Not only had she gotten out of bed, which is a no-no, she got on her brother's Xbox account, another no-no, and purchased a very expensive game package. I wanted to wring her neck and throw the Xbox out the window, but I didn't. I calmly asked her a few questions, let her know the consequences of her actions, and asked her to hand over her Kindle as a temporary punishment until I had time to decide how to move forward. I share this with you because, if I had not had a day of rest the day before, I would not have handled that situation so gracefully. I would have flown off the handle, screamed at her, and probably said or done something I would regret. But because I was well rested, spiritually recharged and refreshed, I had the capacity to handle a stressful situation with God's grace. I wonder how differently that would have gone if I had given in to the temptation to do some work rather than spend time on the couch with Joyce the prior evening.

The truth is, you don't know how important it is to rest until you do it. **There is a better version of you waiting on the other side of your decision to make rest a priority.** What does that person look like? How do they respond? What kind of impact do they make? I can't wait for you to find out!

PSALM 62:1-2 (NIV)
Truly my soul finds rest in God; my salvation comes from him. Truly he is my rock and my salvation; he is my fortress, I will never be shaken.

EXODUS 33:14 (ESV)
My presence will go with you, and I will give you rest.

JOURNAL PROMPTS:

What are some signs that you notice in yourself when you're overworked?

Which day of the week would be a good day for you to rest? If a whole day is not an option, is there a portion of your week, even just a couple hours, that you can set aside to rest?

What is one thing that will be different about you when you are well rested and spiritually refreshed?

_____

_____

_____

_____

_____

_____

_____

_____

_____

_____

_____

_____

WAITING GRACEFULLY

CHAPTER 7

*Let us not become weary in doing good, for at
the proper time we will reap a harvest if we do
not give up.—Galatians 6:9 (NIV)*

Patience is a virtue. Patience is also excruciating. Especially when
your life, your future, your family, or your health are hanging in the
balance. When you are believing God to answer your prayer, it can
easily become all you think about. That issue can begin to consume your
thoughts, disrupt your peace, and shake your soul, as you teeter between
faith and doubt. You know there are people out there that have it worse,
but somehow all you can think about is what you need to happen in your
own life. Self-pity invites you to a party, and before you know it, misery
joins in too.

So, what can we do to find peace in the waiting?

I am currently believing God for some big things to come to pass. I've
been on my knees in prayer and worship, petitioning heaven for answers.
When I stop and meditate long enough on these things I am waiting for,

it can begin to burden me like a ten-ton weight on my shoulders. I begin to doubt if God is hearing me. I wonder when He will decide to make His mighty move. I question whether it is His will. I start acting like a frustrated toddler, throwing mini mental tantrums. I throw up pitiful statements to God like, "Well, I guess I'm just good for nothing. Since you obviously aren't coming through for me." Then I get mad at myself for my ugly heart and allow guilt to seep into my mind. But I know from experience that none of these thoughts are healthy. So, in the waiting, I made a decision, and it has been so incredibly powerful.

I decided to be the answered prayer for others as I wait for mine.

So, I've been keeping my radar up for opportunities to be a blessing to someone else, and they are all around. I've found opportunities to share my platform with those who have a voice and a testimony. I've reached out to the hurting and encouraged them in their time of need. I've given rides, shared coffee, donated supplies, sacrificed time, and gone over and above to be a blessing to others as I wait for God to provide. And every time someone looks me in the eye and sheds a tear of gratitude, my cup overflows. I may not see the Red Sea parting for me, but I've been the staff held out to part it for others. And miracles are happening all around me.

> *Jesus said, "Do unto others as you would have them do unto you."—Luke 6:31*

This doesn't simply mean "Be nice to people." It means that while you're waiting for someone to come through for you, go out of your way to come through for someone else. It means while you're waiting for your big break, find an opportunity to give someone else a break. It means while you're waiting for your healing, pray for healing in someone else's life. It means being the answered prayer for someone else, while you wait patiently for God to bring an answer to yours.

KNEEL ONCE MORE

Elijah, the great prophet of the Lord, wanted rain. It had been three and a half years since he prayed that it would not rain, and it hadn't. Over three years of drought had punished the land and the people for their disobedience to God, but this day, God made it clear to Elijah that it was time for the drought to come to an end.

> *After many days the word of the Lord came to Elijah, in the third year, saying, "Go, show yourself to Ahab, and I will send rain upon the earth." —1 Kings 18:1*

So Elijah climbed Mount Carmel and began to pray.

> *And Elijah went up to the top of Mount Carmel. And he bowed himself down on the earth and put his face between his knees. —1 Kings 18:42*

And nothing happened. Elijah asked his servant to check the sky for signs of rain, and six times he came back with no news. Now, Elijah was a mighty man of God. Much mightier than me, because at this point I might have started complaining. "God, you told me you would bring rain. Now I'm here on a flipping mountain with my head between my knees, and you are nowhere to be found. I've got people relying on me, trusting that you would come through. If you don't send this rain, that king is going to have my head!"

But Elijah knelt once more. And he continued to believe that God would come through.

> *And at the seventh time he said, "Behold, a little cloud like a man's hand is rising from the sea."—1 Kings 18:44*

That little cloud was a sign that a mighty storm was on its way. And it came.

*And in a little while the heavens grew black
with clouds and wind, and there was a great
rain.—1 Kings 18:45 (ESV)*

What are you waiting for? Have you been searching the sky for signs
that your rain is on its way? Have you been complaining to God in the
waiting? Rest assured, friend, God has not turned a deaf ear to you.
His plan is in motion. He is not delayed. He is always on time. Don't
stop praying just because there is no sign of rain. Don't lose heart in the
waiting. Kneel once more. Pray to the God of the harvest. Your little
cloud may be just around the corner!

Dear friend, I know waiting is hard. I know it's painful and you can feel
alone at times, holding up that burden. But, if you can do these things,
you will see miracles happen before your eyes. If you choose to be the
miracle in someone else's life, you will become the hands and feet of Jesus,
and you will experience firsthand the miraculous power of our almighty
God. If you choose to keep praying in faith when you don't see any signs
of change, you will outlast the enemy and see God-sized clouds of blessing
and provision come your way!

GRACE STORY **A VISION FULFILLED**
Sue McDonald

My husband, Chris, had a vision about sixteen years ago of himself
preaching the gospel to thousands of brown-skinned people. He knew
he was called to the nations but had no clue how that would ever play
out. After all, he was just a guy from a small town and really didn't know
anyone who had ever done anything like that. He was pastoring a small
church in our community, and God quickly connected him with a man
in Amarillo. Chris mentored under him and eventually moved our family
there to train under that pastor. For five years, Chris traveled with him
to Honduras, serving and working under that pastor but not feeling
that Honduras was the place God had shown him. After five years of
serving and training, he was asked to go back to his hometown and pastor

the church where he had originally met the Amarillo pastor. He began pastoring there in 2008. He met a missionary from Thailand and went there on a few occasions but again felt these weren't the ones in the vision he had years prior. Then, we had a gentleman start coming to our church who had grown up in the Philippines and had said he would love to take Chris there to teach pastors and leaders.

After much planning, Chris boarded a plane in Chicago and approximately twenty hours later, he landed. When he got off of the plane and saw the faces in the airport, he said he knew, "This is it!" In a few days, he found himself preaching to a sea of faces and knew he had stepped into the vision God had given him sixteen years prior. He knows he will be traveling frequently to the Philippines and living out the call God put on him all those years ago. While Chris waited for his vision to be fulfilled, he served others and helped fulfill theirs. I believe God honored his service.

1 THESSALONIANS 5:17 (KJV)
Pray without ceasing.

1 PETER 1:6–7 (ESV)
In this you rejoice, though now for a little while, if necessary, you have been grieved by various trials, [7] so that the tested genuineness of your faith—more precious than gold that perishes though it is tested by fire—may be found to result in praise and glory and honor at the revelation of Jesus Christ.

2 CORINTHIANS 4:16–18 (ESV)
So we do not lose heart. Though our outer self is wasting away, our inner self is being renewed day by day. [17] For this light momentary affliction is preparing for us an eternal weight of glory beyond all comparison, [18] as we look not to the things that are seen but to the things that are unseen.

JOURNAL PROMPTS:

Who can you bless while you wait?

What prayer have you stopped praying because you got tired of waiting?

_____

_____

_____

_____

_____

_____

HELLO COUNSELOR, GOODBYE STRESS

CHAPTER 8

*I will instruct you and teach you in the way
you should go; I will counsel you with my
loving eye on you.*
—Psalm 32:8

I can handle tough tasks, like mountains of laundry, writing sermons, and praying for the sick. I can handle busy schedules and long to-do lists. Those things don't get to me. What tends to stress me out the most are times when I don't know what to do. Those moments when all is going wrong, and I don't have an answer, a plan, or a solution. That problem begins to reside over my head like a dark looming cloud as my mind marinates on it in turmoil because I don't have control.

I like to have a plan and work the plan. When I have a problem with no solution in sight, I feel like someone just sat me on a roller coaster without a seatbelt, totally out of control.

Maybe you are like me and there are things in your life that stress you out, because you don't know how to handle them. You don't have a solution, and until you do, you are going to worry, marinate on that problem, and lose your mind. There is good news for us, friends! We don't have to rely on our own ideas, strategies, and experiences as we face the unknown.

> *As the heavens are higher than the earth,*
> *so are my ways higher than your ways and my*
> *thoughts than your thoughts.*
> *—Isaiah 55:9 (NIV)*

God has ideas and plans that He wants to share with you, if you will seek Him first. He can come up with solutions to the most complex issues. He can move the largest of mountains. He can settle the fiercest of storms. And all we need to do to access this wisdom, is ask.

> *If any of you lacks wisdom, let him ask God,*
> *who gives generously to all without reproach,*
> *and it will be given him.*
> *—James 1:5 (ESV)*

I have found that the Holy Spirit enjoys helping me plan. He is my helper, my counselor, my comforter, and my adviser. He loves when I sit down, completely at a loss, chat with Him for a moment, and stand back up, ready to charge hell with a squirt gun. He loves giving me ideas and battle plans. And He is so good at it!

You may think it's silly, but I consult the Holy Spirit for even the smallest things. When I don't know what to buy someone for their birthday, I ask Him. When I don't know what creative elements to put into my sermons, I ask Him. When I am having a hard time planning an event, I ask Him.

Why wouldn't we consult the maker of everything when we are planning? To leave Him out is like creating a playbook for football on your own while Vince Lombardi (arguably the greatest football coach of all time) is right by your side, waiting to help.

THE MOST CHAOTIC PLACE ON EARTH

A while back, one of my kids got in trouble on the bus. I know we can all remember back to those days on that big yellow rectangle of chaos. You probably got in trouble at some point too, for sticking your head out the window, throwing spitballs, or smooching in the backseat. But now, as a mom of school-agers, I'm in the place where I have zero control over what happens on big yellow. Every day I place my four greatest blessings on her and pray that nothing bad happens.

Unfortunately, it's not the other kids I am having trouble with this year, it's my own. They're the one pushing, saying mean things, and even going to the extent of biting another kid. Yep. That's my pride and joy, the pastor's kid—the biter. And I was at a complete loss for a solution. I could defend them and give excuses for why they did what they did, but when someone's child is getting bit by mine, they don't care about the excuses. They want the offender disciplined, and I can understand! So when the bus driver waves me over for the fourth time this month, I walk up to big yellow with my head hanging low like a dog to its master. She tells me that my child has been biting again, and she doesn't know what else to do. I wanted so badly to say, "Neither do I!" but I knew that wouldn't help. So I calmly said, "I'll take care of it."

I went home with my biter, my mind racing for ideas. How can I possibly control what this child does on the bus? What type of consequence will be strong enough to get them to control their impulses when they want to whack another kid for saying something mean? I wanted to relate to my kid. There are plenty of times when I want to whack someone. I just happen to have all my filters on at all times. My mind continued to stress as the weight of this problem seemed to fall on my shoulders. I don't want to be the one to solve this! I need an expert! I need someone else to control this child! I am out of ideas!

I didn't respond right away. I took a moment to pray and think. And that's when the Holy Spirit stepped in like my knight in shining armor, handing me His sword and shield, encouraging me to tackle this enemy with wisdom from above. I came up with a plan. And once again, I had regained control of this uncontrollable force of a child. The next day I had my kiddo relay the plan to the bus driver, who was encouraged to hear it. Now it's been a long time since that day, and my little biter has managed to keep their teeth to themselves on the bus!

Praise God, He has answers to our every problem, from parenting to finances to cancer, and everything in between!

MIGHTY MAN OF VALOR

In the Book of Judges, we read about God's people who turn from His ways, reject His commands, and suffer the consequences of those actions. Because of their rebellion, God allowed them to be overtaken by their enemies. The Midianites became their worst nightmare, stealing their crops and land, and forcing them to hide in dens and caves to avoid their enemies. In their turmoil, they turned back to God in prayer.

> *And Israel was brought very low because of Midian. And the people of Israel cried out for help to the Lord.*—Judges 6:6

And, just like the good Father that He is, the Lord provided a man to deliver them, Gideon. An angel appeared to Gideon while he was hiding in a winepress, threshing wheat. The angel called him a "mighty man of valor" and charged him with the task of delivering the Israelites. However, Gideon had some hesitations, as he did not see himself as a "mighty man of valor."

> *And he said to him, "Please, Lord, how can I save Israel? Behold, my clan is the weakest in Manasseh, and I am the least in my father's house."*—Judges 6:15

Maybe you can relate to Gideon. Have you ever been given a task that you don't feel qualified for? Have you tried to pass it off to someone more experienced, smart, or brave? Well, guess what? When God gives an assignment, He's not interested in your excuses or qualifications, and the same was true for Gideon.

The armies of Israel lined up under their new leader, 32,000 men in all. Not bad! But then God asked Gideon to get rid of almost all of them. Reluctantly, Gideon agreed. When all was said and done, he was down to just 300 men. The odds were against them big time, but friend, **when God is involved, odds don't matter.**

You'll have to read the whole story yourself, because the details are entertaining and inspiring. By the grace and guidance of God, Gideon defeated their evil enemies, against all odds, with just 300 men. And the way he did it is fascinating. There is no way that this ordinary man could have formulated such a radical and divine plan. Only the power of God can do that.

Gideon's assignment was much too big for him. His ideas were not enough. He needed help from the Great Counselor, and so do you and I!

GREAT COUNSELOR

What is it that has you all stressed out because you don't know how to solve it? What issue have you lost control over? Rest easy, friend, because you don't have to rely on your own strength. The God of the universe, the omniscient provider of wisdom and the great counselor, is at your side. He loves when you bring Him problems too big for you. He loves giving you ideas and solutions. He loves to hear you lean on Him when you're out of answers.

So hand it over. That problem, event, stressor, or relationship. He has all you need to help you overcome it with grace.

1 PETER 5:7 (NLT)
Give all your worries and cares to God, for he cares about you.

JOHN 14:26 (ESV)
But the Helper, the Holy Spirit, whom the Father will send in my name, he will teach you all things and bring to your remembrance all that I have said to you.

JOURNAL PROMPTS:

In what area of your life could you use some divine wisdom?

Get a moment with the Holy Spirit, turn on some music, and journal your thoughts. God often will show up in your own words as you lean on Him for wisdom.

DROP DEAD DREAD

CHAPTER 9

*All the days of the afflicted are evil, but the
cheerful of heart has a continual feast.*
—*Proverbs 15:15 (ESV)*

What is the one thing in your life that you despise doing? Maybe it's
an event you dread going to—a meeting, a family reunion with the
in-laws, or a difficult conversation that needs to be had. What is it
that you dread?

I can list a bunch of things I do NOT look forward to:
  • dental visits (even though you're the best, Dr. Staten. ☺)
  • working out
  • confrontations
  • going out in the cold
  • diets (food is my love language)

The list goes on and on. But here is the encouraging truth: we don't have
to dread...anything. That's right. Dread is a form of worry, and worry
is not of God. It's like interest paid on trouble before it's due. It's like a

rocking chair. It will keep you busy, but won't get you anywhere. It's a waste of a perfectly good imagination. Enough cheesy analogies? You get the point. Dread is not healthy, and not of God, so let dread drop dead in your life, starting today.

How? I'm so glad you asked.

DOG DAYS

It's the midst of summer in Ohio. The sun is hot, the pools are open, the air conditioning is blowing, and the KIDS ARE HOME from school. I remember back in spring, having this feeling of dread rising up within me. I worried, "How am I going to keep them busy all summer?", "How much am I going to spend in childcare?", "How can I possibly make three meals and two snacks a day for this family of six?", and worst of all, "How am I going to keep this house clean if they never leave it?!"

It's safe to say, this mama of four beautiful blessings was dreading these ninety days of nonstop parenting. But all it took was a change of perspective, and I began to see things differently. This happened as I finished my book, *Finding Strength*, and within it are stories from some incredible people who endured some of the worst trials that life could throw at you. And in speaking to each of them over coffee, by phone, or even email, I began to realize just how precious each day is. I began to look at my life from a fifty-thousand-foot view, and I began to see my children not as little sponges that drain my energy, but precious little people, with whom I only get so much time.

So, I have been taking things a bit slower lately. When they are taking five minutes to get out of the van because they want to bring seven stuffed animals into the store with them, I watch and wait. I take time to notice the silly little expressions on their faces. When they want to tell me a story about the bad dream they had last night, I bend down, look them in the eye, and listen, because one day they won't want to tell me these things.

One night, I was winding down for the evening and decided to get some

R&R time alone in the bath. I set up the candles, a good book, and hot tea, and prepared for some peace and quiet... or so I thought. Five minutes later, Isabella plunged into the bathroom begging me to let her wash my feet (she has a strange foot fetish). I wanted to say, "No honey, this is mommy's time." But, as I remembered how few days we have at this innocent age, I had a change of heart. I let her stay, and we talked about the silliest things as she washed my feet. Then, out of the blue, she said, "Sometimes I see Jesus in the clouds." Wow. What a beautiful image. My baby girl sees Jesus in the clouds. I hate to think that I could have missed that precious moment with my baby girl.

The dread that I once had about this summer has been replaced with a desire to make the most of it. I am not counting down the days until I get my alone time back. I am counting down the days that I have left to make memories with the most important people in my life. I am counting down the years that I have left to influence them. Sure, I have my moments of utter frustration and exhaustion from the long days in the sun, but those moments are fewer and further between than they used to be.

So I play mermaids amidst the mess. I get in the pool with them and let my hair get frizzy and my makeup smear. I spend time and money on things that seem silly to me, but could mean the world to them. These are small sacrifices compared to the reward of memories made.

SILVER LINING

So, dear friend, what are you dreading?

Maybe it's your job. You dread going into work Monday morning. Is there something you can enjoy about your job? Is there something you can do to make it enjoyable for someone else? My former boss once set up a relaxation zone in the break room for us each to take five minutes to unwind during our shift.

Maybe you dread sleepless nights with your infant. What can you enjoy about those twilight moments with your little one? Can you make up a song to sing to them every time they wake? You will remember that song forever. (And when they're eighteen, you can use it to embarrass them at their graduation party.)

Maybe you dread going out, being social, or big events that come with the season. I will tell you the secret to overcoming that. When you walk into that room, or park, or event, walk up to someone, introduce yourself, and start asking questions to get to know them. You'll be amazed at how good you are at socializing when you focus on them and not you!

I once had a mentor named Pat Melcher. She was one of those people who shone like the sun. Her faith moved mountains. Her prayers could knock you off your chair. She lived her entire life surrendered to Jesus. Her home was an open door to ex-convicts for years, and many got saved. She traveled to the prisons, preaching the Good News and delivering monologues that would have you in tears. And near the end of her life, she mentored my husband and I. I get choked up thinking about her, although I know without a doubt she is fully enjoying her new life with Jesus. But one thing I will never forget about Pat was the way she handled adversity. When her appliances broke, she would pray with the repairman who came to fix them. When her car broke down, she'd preach to the salesman. And when she was admitted to the hospital, she turned that whole unit upside down with her joyful spirit and love for Jesus! While most people would be thinking about themselves and their diagnosis, she never showed concern for her body or prognosis. She smiled when she thought of heaven. I remember once when we went to visit her, the first thing out of her mouth was, "Justin, I want you to do my funeral. Come over here and let me tell you about it." Every time she went into the hospital, she prayed with the staff that took care of her. Lord only knows how many lives were changed because of her visits. The last time I saw her, she was lying in her hospital gown while I fed her a chocolate bar. (I know it wasn't healthy, but it's what she requested, and what Pat says, goes!) She looked over to her daughter and said, "Maybe I'll get to see him today" with the most beautiful smile. She was referring to her late husband, who had passed years earlier. She went to be with him shortly after. Pat didn't dread the hospital, the tests, the doctors, the lab results, or even death. She didn't dread anything, because she trusted in God.

I don't know what type of dread you are experiencing, but I happen to believe that there is opportunity to infuse joy into just about any environment if you try!

EXPAND THE GOOD

I once heard it said that everything we focus on expands. I have found this to be true for me, especially with my powerful imagination. When I allow my mind to focus on something coming up in my future, the importance of that event grows and expands, to the point where it feels like the success or failure of that one event will change the course of my life. My mind goes into spaghetti mode and starts weaving in other areas of life that could potentially be affected by the outcome of this event, and before you know it, I'm a ball of stress. I can begin to dread the near future, exaggerating the possibilities and expecting the worst. Allow me to give you an example. Join me inside my head for a moment.

It was a nice spring day, and our family was heading into town for some quality time at the local festival. Justin looked down from driving and noticed he had missed a call from one of our church members. This was not someone who called often. "I wonder what he wanted?" I asked. And then began the trail of negative thoughts. I wondered if something bad had happened in his family. We get a lot of calls in the midst of people's tragedy. I imagined him calling to say he was upset at us for something. Then I began to think back through the last few weeks, trying to figure out if I had done something to make their family mad. I even went so far as to think they were calling to tell us they were leaving the church. I rehearsed how that conversation would go. All of this sped through my head in a matter of two minutes, long enough for Justin to call him back and find out that our fundraiser order was ready for pickup. Uh huh. That's all it was. I know I'm crazy, but that's an example of what our minds can do if we allow them to run wild in the wrong direction. Maybe you have a tough conversation coming up, and you have been rehearsing in your mind all day, expecting the worst. Maybe you have a doctor's appointment coming up, and you're imagining getting the worst news possible. Maybe you are in the midst of a difficult situation and you're not sure which way things are going to go, but you continue to let your mind imagine the worst outcome. Listen, friend, I understand. I am just as guilty as anyone for letting my mind run wild in the wrong direction, but we cannot afford to live that way. It will only make us miserable.

> *Who of you by worrying can add a single hour*
> *to your life?—Luke 12:25 (NIV)*

Jesus knew that people like you and me would be prone to worry, and He gave us those words to live by, before psychologists or therapists even existed. Our Creator knew that worrisome thoughts would attack our minds and steal our joy if we let them. Now researchers know that over ninety percent of the things we worry about never even happen. Ninety percent! That means you are wasting all that mental energy worrying about something that is never going to happen! And what about the other ten percent? Well, I will tell you this: your worrying is not going to make that outcome any better. **Bad things do happen in life every now and then, but worrying about them in advance doesn't make them any easier to deal with.** So, you might as well live your life free from worry!

Our lives are rarely changed by one event. Our lives are made up of lots and lots of little events and decisions that determine our future. But in the moment, when our minds are focused on that one thing, it expands in our lives and consumes our thoughts. So how do we take back control of our thoughts and get a better, healthier perspective on life, so we can live more peacefully?

I'll tell you my secret. I learned it from someone much smarter than myself, who has a degree in psychology. The secret is this: When you notice your mind drifting off into "worst case scenario" land, ask yourself, "What is the best-case scenario in this situation?" Allow your imagination to go in the opposite direction, even to the opposite extreme. So, when your boss sends you an email that reads "I want to see you in my office at

2:00," your mind may automatically think the worst ("I'm getting fired"), but tell it to think the best ("I'm getting a raise of double my salary"). Then, to bring your mind back to center and tell yourself that the reality will most likely be in the middle of those two outcomes. You're probably not getting fired. You're probably not getting a raise of double your salary. Something in the middle is the most likely outcome.

Everything you focus on will expand in your mind, and wherever your mind goes, you follow. So don't waste your mental energy and your precious time on this earth worrying about worst-case scenarios. Don't overestimate the effects of one event on your future. **You serve a really big God who can turn things around, make up for lost time, steer you back in the right direction when you get off course, and bring something good from even the most difficult circumstances.** And even when those tough times come, you will not be alone. Your Heavenly Father will be right there by your side, comforting you, strengthening you, and equipping you to make it through.

So tell dread that it can drop dead today, and get on living your life!

PHILIPPIANS 4:8 (NIV)

Finally, brothers and sisters, whatever is true, whatever is noble, whatever is right, whatever is pure, whatever is lovely, whatever is admirable—if anything is excellent or praiseworthy—think about such things.

What have you been dreading lately? Why?

What is the most positive outcome you can imagine happening in that situation? Close your eyes and envision it coming to pass.

Think on positive thoughts, positive dreams and goals, and positive relationships in your life.
- what are you most looking forward to right now?
- who in your life do you appreciate? Thank God for them
- what do you enjoy doing? Schedule a time to do that in the near future.

_____

_____

_____

_____

_____

_____

_____

_____

_____

_____

_____

PURSUIT OF HAPPINESS

CHAPTER 10

*"We hold these truths to be self-evident, that all
men are created equal, that they are endowed
by their Creator with certain unalienable
Rights, that among these are Life, Liberty and
the pursuit of Happiness."*
—*The Declaration of Independence*

Happiness. How is your pursuit going? Have you discovered the secret to this elusive feeling? Have you found the source of true happiness in your life? Or perhaps you, like myself and many others, have successfully discovered many paths that do NOT lead to happiness. Maybe you find yourself on a path similar to Dorothy, who thought she was heading to her promised land, only to get there and realize that the Emerald City wasn't all it was cracked up to be and found herself fighting the same enemy there as she did in the forest. Well, regardless of where you are in this pursuit of happiness, I have some encouragement for you that is certain to help you in your journey.

LAND OF OPPORTUNITY

Our country is affectionately called the "Land of Opportunity," a place where we pride ourselves on the freedoms we have as citizens. Here in the US, you can choose to be anything you want to be. You can choose to go to college, or begin a career. You can choose to marry or stay single. You can choose to change career paths, start a business, volunteer, or start your own non-profit organization. The possibilities are endless. So, we all begin this pursuit toward the life we envision as ideal, the life that is sure to make us happy. But what if the path we are on isn't leading us to happiness? And how are we to know whether or not this journey we are on will lead us to fulfillment? As I will explain here in a moment, it is my personal opinion that many Americans are on a deceiving path—one that appears to lead to happiness, but in actuality only leads to more dissatisfaction.

What is happiness? *Psychology Today* explains it this way:

> *"More than simply positive mood, happiness is a state of well-being that encompasses living a good life—that is, with a sense of meaning and deep satisfaction."*
> —Psychology Today (www.psychologytoday.com)

If happiness comes from living a good life, then it would be crucial to identify what exactly a good life consists of. I believe we all envision "the good life" a little differently, depending on our own personal goals, but there are probably a few similarities: health, prosperity, love, and purpose. Sadly though, as we pursue happiness, we typically narrow our focus toward the prosperity piece of the puzzle. Many people believe that if they can just get to that next level of income, status, promotion, or material wealth, they will finally experience that sense of well-being we're all searching for. But, I can tell you, they won't find it there.

Many people who the world would identify as "successful" would admit that ***success doesn't satisfy***. With every level of success, there is another goal, another level to hit, another achievement ahead that is sure to be the one to bring satisfaction. It will never be enough. If you're not convinced of this, ask the most successful person you know how satisfied they are with their level of success. I bet they have their sights set on the next goal.

A few summers ago I was out boating on the Atlantic Ocean on a beautiful summer day with family and friends. We were cruising along the coast, admiring the scenery, when one of my friends stated something that took me aback. Most people would describe this man as successful. He was a wealthy business owner with a beautiful wife and kids, a large home with land, several nice vehicles, and enough time and money to take vacations just about anywhere he chose. But as this man took notice of the gorgeous mansions along the Atlantic Coast, he felt dissatisfied and stated, "What are we doing wrong in life that we can't have that?"

Prosperity, when it comes to material wealth, will never satisfy. And yet, too often people establish their plans and paths toward creating more income so they can buy more things, so they can go more places, so they can have more happiness.

TIME TO CHANGE COURSE

So what is the answer, or the key to happiness, as some call it? Well, a few moments ago we described the good life as this: health, prosperity, love, and purpose. I'm not here to be your health coach. There are much more qualified people to do that. Prosperity has proven to lead to a hunger for more. So we are left with pursuing love and purpose.

What if we, starting today, changed course in our pursuit and allowed our paths to be directed by love and purpose? I believe that we will find along the way that health and prosperity will follow. After all, God is love, and as we pursue Him, He promises to give us all things needed to live a healthy life. Don't believe me? Read for yourself!

Anyone who does not love does not know God,
because God is love.—1 John 4:8 (ESV)

> *Therefore I tell you, do not be anxious about your life,*
> *what you will eat or what you will drink, nor about your*
> *body, what you will put on. Is not life more than food, and*
> *the body more than clothing?* *²⁶ Look at the birds of the*
> *air: they neither sow nor reap nor gather into barns, and*
> *yet your heavenly Father feeds them. Are you not of more*
> *value than they?* *²⁷ And which of you by being anxious*
> *can add a single hour to his span of life?* *²⁸ And why are*
> *you anxious about clothing? Consider the lilies of the field,*
> *how they grow: they neither toil nor spin,* *²⁹ yet I tell you,*
> *even Solomon in all his glory was not arrayed like one of*
> *these.* *³⁰ But if God so clothes the grass of the field, which*
> *today is alive and tomorrow is thrown into the oven, will*
> *he not much more clothe you, O you of little faith?* *³¹*
> *Therefore do not be anxious, saying, "What shall we eat?"*
> *or "What shall we drink?" or "What shall we wear?"³² For*
> *the Gentiles seek after all these things, and your heavenly*
> *Father knows that you need them all.—Matthew 6:25–32*

(And now for the grand finale…)

> *But seek first the kingdom of God and his righteousness,*
> *and all these things will be added to you.—Matthew 6:33*
> *(ESV, emphasis mine)*

As we pursue our Creator, and the things He deems important in life, we will discover true happiness and contentment doesn't come from a status, income bracket, or material item. It comes from fulfilling our God-given purpose.

WHAT IS MY PURPOSE?

This is the question so many Christians wrestle with as they pursue God. They see people who have started churches, led non-profits, written

books, and produced albums, and they question whether or not God
has given them a unique purpose. I will tell you this: **your purpose in
life isn't a one-time achievement of any kind.** My purpose in life isn't
to start Impact City Church. That is simply one of the avenues God is
using me through. My purpose in life isn't to speak, although I do love
preaching God's Word with a passion. My purpose in life isn't to author
books, although I find it very fulfilling. My purpose is to love God and
love His people, and the ways in which I do that vary from season to
season. And your purpose is the same.

> *"Teacher, which is the great commandment in the Law?"*
> *³⁷ And he said to him, "You shall love the Lord your God
> with all your heart and with all your soul and with all
> your mind. ³⁸ This is the great and first commandment.
> ³⁹ And a second is like it: You shall love your neighbor as
> yourself. ⁴⁰ On these two commandments depend all the
> Law and the Prophets."—Matthew 22:36–40*

Your purpose is not an event, an achievement, or a goal that can be
attained in a period of time. Your purpose began the moment you were
born and will continue until your last breath. There is not a day that goes
by that you do not have a God-given purpose. Your purpose is bigger
than you can imagine and stretches farther than you will ever know until
heaven. **Your purpose is fulfilled with each small action of love, care,
and service toward another.** It cannot be measured and very rarely is
recognized publicly. Your purpose is to love your God, and to love His
people.

When we allow our lives to be directed by anything other than love,
we are off-course and certain to experience sadness, dissatisfaction, and
frustration. Sadly, many people find themselves there, because they have
been pursuing happiness down the wrong path. I have even found myself,
on some days, in this position.

Justin and I have a standing weekly date night. We were recently on one
of these dates, and I found myself down in the dumps. I had no real

explanation for it. We ate great food. We listened to my favorite music, and he even took me to see the prettiest Christmas lights in town. But I still ended the night feeling "blah." You know the feeling. I'm not sure what it is, but it definitely isn't happiness. To add insult to injury, I felt guilty for being so "blah." I felt like I should have been happy. I should have been a joy to be around. I should have been grateful. But instead, I was a bump on a log. And the truth was, I had spent the whole day trying to be happy. But I did so by pursuing my own personal happiness, and I pray you know by now, that is not the way. Throughout the day, I had my alone time, I rested, I went on a date, I saw pretty things, and yet I still wasn't happy. If that night did anything, it proved to me once more that happiness is not found in serving yourself; it is found in serving others. So the next day I did just that. I pursued God in prayer first thing, and I spent the day expressing His love to others. I served. I cared. I went above and beyond, and I found my happiness again.

If we are honest, we are all a bit selfish. It is natural to pursue a life that satisfies our own desires, wants, and goals. We are trained by society to look out for number one and believe in ourselves. But what if society is wrong? **What if the true key to happiness isn't putting ourselves first, but putting others first?** As I observe some of the happiest people in my life, it is those who live their lives in service to others.

My friend, Kelly, is one of the happiest people I know. She doesn't just give the illusion of being happy by putting on a front; she actually exudes joy from the inside out, and it lands on everyone she encounters. Whenever you leave her presence, you feel a bit more joyful. And yet, Kelly doesn't pursue her own happiness at all. In fact, she spends her every day, 24/7, serving others. She is our pastor's assistant at church, responding to every need that comes through the church and from Justin and I. She works on the clock and off the clock serving our church. I always say, "If anyone has a longer to-do list than me, it's Kelly." She is the wife of our worship pastor, Ron, and she serves him in such a way that every wife should aspire to. She is also the mother of five young children, who tug and pull on her every ounce of energy at home from early morning through the middle of the night. Kelly truly lives her life poured out, and yet she carries not an ounce of bitterness within her. I believe that the secret to her happiness comes from her pursuit to love God and love others.

In contrast, I know many unhappy people who live unsatisfied, frustrated, and depressed lives, but continue only to seek their own happiness, thinking that maybe someone or something will come along and meet their needs. Sadly, they will never find true happiness until they stop pursuing their own selfish desires.

Every day we are given the option to pursue our own happiness, or to pursue true happiness through loving God and loving others. Disclaimer: this doesn't eliminate the need for self-care. I still do date night every week to keep my marriage strong. I still rest daily and weekly. I still do things I enjoy and take good care of myself. Because I know my health—spiritually, mentally, emotionally, and physically—is crucial to helping others. But I don't allow too much time to go by without pouring out God's love on someone else, because that is my purpose, and that is my pursuit.

So, I will end this chapter the way I began it. Happiness. How is your pursuit going?

SCRIPTURE STUDY:

PSALM 16:11 (ESV)
You make known to me the path of life;
in your presence there is fullness of joy;
at your right hand are pleasures forevermore.

GALATIANS 6:7 (ESV)
Do not be deceived: God is not mocked, for whatever one sows, that will
he also reap.

GALATIANS 6:8 (ESV)
Whoever sows to please their flesh, from the flesh will reap destruction;
whoever sows to please the Spirit, from the Spirit will reap eternal life.

JOURNAL PROMPTS:

What does happiness look like to you?

How can you pursue happiness by serving others this week?

_____

_____

_____

_____

_____

_____

_____

_____

_____

_____

GRACE FOR A CHANGE

CHAPTER 11

Whenever the cloud lifted from above the tent, the Israelites set out; wherever the cloud settled, the Israelites encamped.
[18] At the Lord's command the Israelites set out, and at his command they encamped. As long as the cloud stayed over the tabernacle, they remained in camp.
—Numbers 9:17–18 (NIV)

"I can't do all of this anymore!" I yelled from my bedroom. Although nobody could hear me, it felt good to get it out. It was spring of 2015, and I knew it was time for a change, but it seemed like everything I was doing was important. As all my responsibilities spiraled around in my stressed-out head, I felt trapped in the chaos. It seemed like there was no way out. We needed the income from my job. The church needed me to minister. My kids needed food and clothing. The house needed cleaned. My son needed homeschooled. And all of it was my responsibility! After screaming to nobody, I decided to get some wise counsel on the situation. Even if there wasn't an answer, maybe I would feel better just knowing somebody understood my predicament.

After a few minutes of venting over the phone, my friend gave me some very wise advice. She said, "There is something in your life that God has not graced." I asked her to explain. She went on to open my eyes to this idea of changing grace. *Sometimes God will give us the grace to accomplish something for a season, but not forever.* When your time in that season is finished, He will lift the grace and you will feel the discomfort. For me personally, God's grace had lifted on my time homeschooling my son. And as I reflected on this, it was clear that she was right. It was the one area that seemed to be a constant struggle. When I began homeschooling, it was great. He soared through the curriculum; we made memories, did crafts, and took lots of field trips. But lately, every day was a struggle. God had graced it for a season, but that season was over.

That was years ago. Since then, I have had to ask myself this question at least once a year: *What am I doing right now that God has not graced me to do?*

YOU'RE NOT THAT SPECIAL

When my plate gets too full and I find myself burning the candles at both ends, it's time for a recalibration. It's time to ask God where He has graced me for this season and to be strong enough to remove the responsibilities that I know aren't necessary. This can be extremely difficult. Especially if you're the hero type like myself. You may feel like everyone needs you all the time. You may wonder how they will survive without you. It may seem like you can't take one day off without the world coming to an end, but I have some sobering truth for you: you're not that special.

Now before you throw this book across the room, allow me to explain. Of course you are a special person, created by God to do great things, but the minute you start to believe that the world will end if you take one day off, you're off balance.

Recently I was tossing up the idea of skipping a church event. In this season, when the church is growing leaps and bounds and new people are attending every week, I feel the pressure to try to connect to each new person and ensure their experience is a good one. We had an event coming up that offered new guests an opportunity to meet the pastors, get to know the church culture, and get involved. In the past, I tried not to miss these, because I felt like my presence there made a difference. But this particular week I was overwhelmed. The responsibilities were piling up, but I still felt obligated to go to this event. As I drove, I felt God relieve the pressure with these words: "You aren't that special. You don't need to be at everything. Your presence does make a difference, but only if you're in your grace."

Friend, you're not helping anyone by showing up to something stressed out and overwhelmed. You're not helping your coworkers by picking up shifts for them if you're going to complain about it or hold it over their head. You're not helping your children by taking them on a million "family fun" trips, if you're going to be yelling and reprimanding the whole time. **You don't have to do everything you think you have to do.**

WELCOME TO YOUR BREAKING POINT

Sometimes God will make you so uncomfortable that you will be forced to make a change. Just last year my husband, Justin, experienced this. For four years, he was a bivocational pastor. He worked three days a week as a project manager for the federal government, and six days a week for the church. Working with two laptops going at a time became the norm for him. I would sometimes find him facedown in one of them, snoozing at his desk because he was so tired. I remember him falling asleep during family games in the evening out of pure exhaustion. It got really funny when he mixed up his responsibilities and sent an email to his whole department that invited all government employees to a "Worship Workshop." For a while, Justin experienced God's amazing, empowering grace to work both jobs. He wanted to be a full-time pastor, but he knew he was making the right choice for his family and the church to work his government job. It provided great pay and great benefits for us and relieved the pressure of the church to provide for our family. But there came a day when that grace lifted. I can't tell you exactly when it was, but it became clear the day he broke down. We were on our back deck chatting when I could tell he was beginning to break. For the first time in our marriage, he was beyond his ability. He had always carried everything so well on his broad shoulders. It would amaze me at times to watch him hold it all up with such grace, confidence, and zeal. I would often tell him, "I don't know how you do it, Jus. I could never carry the weight that you carry." I know now that he was doing it by the grace of God, but when the grace lifted, it became too much for him to bear alone. As I watched him break down under the pressure, I reminded him of this truth: **Sometimes it takes a breaking point to force us to make a change.** I said, "Welcome to your breaking point. It's time to quit your job." A few weeks later, Justin turned in his resignation letter to DFAS. It was a really difficult decision for him to make, especially without knowing how God was going to provide, but when you know that you know that you know that God is asking you to do something, you must step out in faith.

Every time God asked us to do something great, it required great faith. So, by faith, Justin went full-time into ministry. At that time, we were heading into summer (a low season for churches typically), with a HUGE pay cut, no insurance, and all the while making preparations to officially adopt our daughter, which would cost $2500. It didn't make sense! Who in their right mind would take that kind of risk? Are you ready to hear the miracle? That month, before we received Justin's final paycheck from DFAS, a couple handed us an envelope after church, full of cash. Enough money to supplement Justin's income for the rest of the summer! Come on, Jesus! When you listen for God's prompting, and move when He says to move, He comes through!

When Justin stepped out of his job, he stepped back into God's grace. He walked a little lighter, smiled a little more, and had more energy for the important things in life. He became the man who I had missed for a while. I wonder where we would be if he hadn't broken down and gotten so uncomfortable that he was forced to make a change? I praise God for lifting the grace in that area so that we could experience His grace in a greater way now.

MOVING WITH THE CLOUD

This idea of moving with the grace of God is no new thing. In the Old Testament, we can read about a time when God's presence dwelled in the Tabernacle. The Israelites, God's people, built a tabernacle by His command, so that God could have a holy place to dwell near their camp. This became a place of worship, sacrificial ceremonies, and communication with God. And the manifestation of God's presence over the Tabernacle would come in the form of a cloud by day and fire by night. But when God wanted them to move, the cloud or fire would lift away from the tent. When they saw this, the Israelites knew it was time to move.

> *Whenever the cloud lifted from above the tent, the Israelites set out; wherever the cloud settled, the Israelites encamped. 18 At the Lord's command the Israelites set out, and at his command they encamped. As long as the cloud stayed over the tabernacle, they remained in camp.*
> *—Numbers 9:17–18 (NIV)*

Man, wouldn't it be nice if God gave us a physical cloud to guide us in the right direction? Wouldn't it be great if we could see or hear Him with our natural senses? Well, we may not have a cloud or fire, but we have something greater. We have the guidance of the Holy Spirit within us.

> *These things I have spoken to you while I am still with you. 26 But the Helper, the Holy Spirit, whom the Father will send in my name, he will teach you all things and bring to your remembrance all that I have said to you. 27 Peace I leave with you; my peace I give to you. Not as the world gives do I give to you. Let not your hearts be troubled, neither let them be afraid.—John 14:25–27 (ESV)*

The Holy Spirit is our guide, giving us peace as an indicator of where God's grace lies. When I am counseling people who are trying to make decisions, I encourage them to pray about the decision, and follow peace. One decision may sound right, but deep down you know it's not the right choice. The other decision might not look good on paper, but feels right in your spirit. That's the guidance of the Holy Spirit.

When Justin made the decision to quit his job, it didn't make any sense on paper, but we had a peace in our spirits that it was the right choice, and God would come through. Sometimes it feels like there is no peace in our lives, and that is a warning sign that we are living outside of God's grace. This may mean it's time to realign our schedules with our priorities. It may mean we need to obey God's command to rest. It may mean removing something from our plate. It may mean saying "no" more often to opportunities. Or, for you, it may mean saying "yes" to the thing God is calling you to do, which brings me to my next point.

FRUSTRATION, DEPRESSION, AND THE LIKE...

Living outside of the grace of God can be the most frustrating place on earth. I can't imagine the consequences the Israelites would have faced if they hadn't followed the cloud and fire of God's presence when it guided them to move. They may have never made it to the Promised Land.

So, what about you? Do you feel like you're living in the wilderness, with no cloud to guide you? Do you feel frustrated about where you are in life? Do you have dreams of doing something with purpose, but feel so far from accomplishing them? I have seen far too many people with great purpose choose to stay behind when God's grace is leading them ahead. They choose what seems safe, rather than what requires faith. They choose the road well-paved, with a predictable end, and find that road leads only to emptiness. **You will never be fulfilled outside of the grace of God.** And if you stay there long enough, you'll be accompanied by feelings of hopelessness and depression. Listen, I hate to be the bearer of bad news, but I want God's best for you, and I've seen too many people living in the darkness of their own making. God gave them a light, an idea, a dream, but fear or insecurity kept them from fulfilling it, and the light moved on.

BUT! There is good news! You can step into God's grace for your life at any time and experience the fullness of His presence! You can go back to that thing God asked you to do and start today taking steps toward it. We serve a gracious God; when we take steps toward Him, He begins taking steps back toward us (James 4:8). That cloud of peace and light may seem far away, but one step in the right direction may be all it takes to bring it back to you.

The Israelites made mistake after mistake, but God continued to offer forgiveness and grace, and He's still doing it today. If you find yourself saying, "I can't do all of this anymore," it may be time to hand God your overflowing plate and ask Him what needs to be removed. If you find yourself living in darkness or depression, it may be time to ask yourself, "What is the last thing God asked me to do?" and go back to that thing. There is no better place to live than within God's will for your life. I pray you find that place and experience the peace of God that surpasses all human understanding!

SCRIPTURE STUDY:

JAMES 4:8 (ESV)
Draw near to God, and he will draw near to you.

PSALM 119:105 (ESV)
Your word is a lamp to my feet and a light to my path.

JOHN 14:26 (ESV)
But the Helper, the Holy Spirit, whom the Father will send in my name, he will teach you all things and bring to your remembrance all that I have said to you.

JOURNAL PROMPTS:

Write down all of your responsibilities, then pray about each one. Ask God to reveal any areas in which His Grace has lifted.

Think back to the last thing God asked you to do. Did you follow His lead or resist? What is one thing you can begin to do today to get back on track in that area?

_____

_____

_____

_____

_____

_____

_____

_____

_____

SILENCING KINGS

CHAPTER 12

*Your servant has struck down both lions and
bears, and this uncircumcised Philistine shall
be like one of them, for he has defied the
armies of the living God.—1 Samuel 17:36*

Are you facing a giant in your life? Do you feel alone in that battle?
Or, even worse, do you feel as if the people around you are making
the battle harder to fight?

You may have heard the saying, *"Everyone is fighting a battle you know
nothing about. Be kind, always."* I think we would all agree with that,
especially when we are the ones feeling attacked. Sometimes I want to say,

"I am fighting a battle you know nothing about. Be nice to me."

I happen to believe that life is hard enough without the criticism and
correction of others. I happen to believe that our own personal giants are
tough enough to fight, without the added pressure, guilt, and attacks from
those around us.

When I feel this way, I remember David, who not only faced a giant, but did so without support.

The scene was intense—the giant taunting the armies of the living God of Israel. The army was shaking in their boots, not one soldier brave enough to face Goliath. Then came David, anointed by God for such a time as this, but not adequate, experienced, or respected by men. When he spoke up, rebuking Goliath and offering to defeat him, he received the opposite of support. You would think that the army would be grateful. You would think that his brother would be proud, but instead, David was accused of having an "evil heart."

> *When Eliab, David's oldest brother, heard him speaking with the men, he burned with anger at him and asked, "Why have you come down here? And with whom did you leave those few sheep in the wilderness? I know how conceited you are and how wicked your heart is; you came down only to watch the battle."—1 Samuel 17:28*

David's time had come. His giant awaited, threatening his life. In this moment, I'm sure David had a mental battle stirring in his own mind. I'm sure he was well aware of the odds against him. I'm sure he wondered if he would make it out of this battle alive. I'm sure he was already hushing the voices in his mind telling him to turn back. What he needed most in this moment was a little encouragement. He probably could have used some "atta boys." But, instead, he was accused of being evil and selfish. Apparently this was not a new thing for David, though, because his response indicates that this wasn't the first time his older brother had criticized him.

> *"Now what have I done?" said David. "Can't I even speak?"—1 Samuel 17:29*

David ignored the criticism of his brother and was brought into the presence of King Saul, who only made matters worse.

David said to Saul, "Let no one lose heart on account of
this Philistine; your servant will go and fight him."
Saul replied, "You are not able to go out against this
Philistine and fight him; you are only a young man, and he
has been a warrior from his youth."—1 Samuel 17:32–33

As David, our brave underdog, faced the greatest challenge of his life, he was met only with criticism, warnings, and bad advice. But somehow, amidst his own inner turmoil and the external attacks of those around him, he kept moving toward his destiny.

We all know the end of the story. Goliath is defeated, the Israelites are saved, and little David becomes a hero.

So, friend, what does this have to do with us? Two things:

1. WHEN YOU ARE FACING GIANTS, MOVING TOWARD YOUR DESTINY, YOU WILL HAVE CRITICS.

Everyone has an opinion. They are entitled to it. But you don't have to accept their opinion as truth. You can move on with your destiny, despite their attempts to derail you.

2. DON'T BE THE ELIAB

I would LOVED to have seen the expression on Eliab's face when his little brother, who he tried to send back to the sheep, put Goliath on his face! I wonder if Eliab tried to take credit for David's success. I wonder if he said something like, "I believed in you all along, little bro." I don't know, but I know this: I don't want to be the Eliab in someone else's life. I don't want to be the critical, mean, unbelieving voice when someone really needs encouragement. I want to be like Jonathan, King Saul's son, who became a voice of encouragement and protected David from harm. I want to be the one who believes in people before there is any evidence of success. I want to be a pressure-relief valve for others in a world full of pressure.

MY ELIABS

When I first started into ministry, the voices of critics really affected me. There were—and still are—many who believed women don't have a place behind the pulpit. In the beginning, they tried to get me to step down. Some tried to be easy on me, with softer words like, "You should really focus on the home, and let Justin do the leading." Some were much more hurtful, sending letters to the church and commenting on our Facebook posts. They despised the sight of me in church leadership. After all, I am a female, and females can only teach children and sing songs. (FYI, I tried to join the worship team, but apparently you have to be able to sing or play an instrument, and they said cowbell doesn't count.) I have a lot of things I could say to the critics, backed up by Biblical reasons I believe women have a place in church leadership, but that's all another book for another time. The bottom line is, I had many Eliabs, and still do today. They want to see me go back to the fields and tend my sheep. They want to see me fail. But the voice I must listen to above all others is the Holy Spirit, and He calls me into places even I am intimidated to go. He leads me beyond my own capabilities. He stretches me and pushes me out of my comfort zone and into His grace. And if His grace ever moved, and His voice called me out of this role, I would follow, but so far He has not. I've never fit the "perfect pastor" mold, but I'm making a way for those who will come after me to follow, and I've made a commitment to God to never underestimate a person just because they seem "small." God has, and will, used small people to do big things!

So, friends, if you are facing a giant today, and friends or family are adding insult to injury, be encouraged. You don't need their approval to do what God is calling you to do. Yes, it would be great if you were surrounded by cheerleaders, but more than likely, you are surrounded by Eliabs and Sauls. Keep on keepin' on. You were created for something great.

And lastly, make a decision today to be more like Jonathan and less like Eliab for your friends and family. When you are tempted to correct, judge, gossip, criticize, or warn, instead choose to uplift, encourage, and strengthen them. Chances are, they are already facing a battle in their mind, and the last thing they need is another attack.

1 TIMOTHY 4:12 (ESV)
Let no one despise you for your youth, but set the believers an example in speech, in conduct, in love, in faith, in purity.

1 TIMOTHY 6:20–21 (ESV)
O Timothy, guard the deposit entrusted to you. Avoid the irreverent babble and contradictions of what is falsely called "knowledge," [21] for by professing it some have swerved from the faith.

2 TIMOTHY 1:7 (ESV)
For God gave us a spirit not of fear but of power and love and self-control.

JOURNAL PROMPTS:

Who is your Eliab?

How have you allowed their words to hinder your life?

Pray for that person, then decide to stop letting the voices of critics be stronger than the voice of the Holy Spirit in your life.

_____

_____

_____

_____

_____

_____

_____

_____

GRACE FOR WEIRDOS

CHAPTER 13

Before I formed you in the womb I knew you,
and before you were born I consecrated you; I
appointed you a prophet to the nations.
—Jeremiah 1:5 (ESV)

D o you ever feel like an outcast in society? Does the ever-changing world leave you feeling behind? Do you wonder if maybe God made a mistake when He put you here, in this era, among these people?

I sometimes feel as if I would have been better suited for a different century, one in which people lived slower-paced lives, tending to gardens, playing tag in the yard, riding horses into town, and relaxing on the front porch for hours. I look around today at this concrete jungle, full of robots staring blankly into their phones all day, kids pressured to do everything at an earlier age, and families running in different directions, and I wonder why God put me here. The more I try to keep up with the trends, the more I realize I will never keep up. I finally get the hang of one fad in time for it to be outdated. I get used to one device just in time for technology gurus to create the next overpriced craze. I feel like a stranger in this world sometimes. I feel like there is nobody else in the world who thinks like I do. I wonder if I'm the only one whose imagination runs wild and whose mind goes a little on the crazy side at times. I wonder if I'm the only one who gets freaked out at the thought of eternity. I wonder if I'm the only one who tries to understand everything and has a tendency to think deeper than my human mind can comprehend, leaving me feeling overwhelmed and anxious.

This is just me being real with you. Sometimes, quite frankly, I just feel like a weirdo.

We all want to know that we are unique, but nobody wants to feel like a weirdo. Nobody wants to feel like this world has moved on and left them behind. Nobody wants to feel alone in their strange thoughts, desires, and dreams. The truth is, God did create you uniquely, for a unique purpose. There isn't anyone just like you. You are special, not in the condescending way that some might use that word. You are special to God, and your body, mind, soul, and spirit carry a unique combination that is worth more than gold to your Creator.

> *For we are God's masterpiece. He has created*
> *us anew in Christ Jesus, so we can do the good*
> *things he planned for us long ago.*
> *—Ephesians 2:10 (NLT)*

Now here is the comforting part: you are not alone. You may be the only you on this planet, but you are not alone. Each and every one of us has something that makes us a bit different than the person next to us, and that's the way it's meant to be. But in the same respect, there is so much about us that's alike. We all have strengths. We all have weaknesses. We all have highs. We all have lows. We all experience pain. We all experience love. **We are not as different as we may think, but the differences that do exist are for a great purpose.**

God has placed a unique grace on your life, for this season. He has given you natural strengths, but in addition to those, He has endowed you with supernatural strengths, by His great grace, and those strengths can differ from season to season.

> *From His fullness we have all received grace*
> *upon grace.—John 1:16 (ESV)*

Sadly, for many, that supernatural grace, God's empowerment in our lives, gets suppressed, lying dormant inside the heart of a beaten-down, hurting child of God. **The painful opinions, words, and actions of others have trumped the voice of their Creator who calls them.** They have allowed comparison to hinder their gifts. In their attempt to be like someone else, they lose their true self, and their unique purpose along with it.

Friend, I beg you, don't let another day go by without breaking free from the chains of comparison and insecurity. There is too much at stake when we live our lives imprisoned by the pressure of others. You may not be like everyone else, and there is a GREAT reason for that.

TOOTHPASTE FOR LUNCH

My sweet daughter, Mckenzie, is ten years old. When I look at her, I wonder what I did to deserve a child so sweet. She has the kindest heart I've ever seen. She is as soft and gentle as a flower, but also has a love and compassion for others that is strong enough to stand up and fight for the little guy. She cares about people in a way that seems long gone in today's world. She is special, no doubt. What pains me, though, is to watch her allow the words and opinions of others to make her feel inferior. I hate when she comes home in tears telling me how another student made fun of her. I hate to see her sweet spirit being taken advantage of by mean kids. I don't want her to change, but I wish it didn't hurt her so much to be herself. I pray every night that God will protect her innocence and her purity. I remind her all the time that kindness is strong, and she should never stop being kind just because someone else is mean. Sometimes, though, she just feels so different than the others, and it makes her wish she could be like everyone else.

Mckenzie has to eat gluten-free, which limits her diet. So every day she eats the same thing for lunch. She already feels different. Recently I had to ask her to start brushing her teeth after lunch, because she had a mouthful of cavities and infections. Now, she's the only gluten-free kid in class and the only one who has toothpaste in her lunchbox. Last week the kids started laughing when they saw it and said, "She's eating toothpaste for lunch!" That crushed her gentle heart. I was tempted to go to lunch with her and slap some sense into those bullies! Mama bear wanted to protect her little cub. But then I got a better idea. After a chat with another mom, the problem was solved. Mckenzie got a brushing buddy to join her after lunch. Not only did she feel less alone, some other kids saw what they were doing and wanted to join the club!

When I look at Mckenzie, I don't see a weirdo. I see a one-of-a-kind world-changer. I see a beautiful girl with a beautiful heart. I see someone who is going to make a significant difference in this world. But sometimes she doesn't see herself the way I do. She hears the voices of her peers. She listens to the insecure thoughts in her head. She allows the pressures of the crowd to make her feel inferior. But it is my goal to get her to see herself the way I do, the way God sees her. I want her to know what I know— that she doesn't have to worry about what other people think. She doesn't have to listen to their mean words. She doesn't have to feel inferior. She is amazing! I want her to walk into school with a God-size confidence and be the special girl that He has created her to be.

I wonder, friend, if you could use a dose of God's thoughts about you. I wonder if you have allowed the voices of others to be louder than the voice of the Holy Spirit in your life. I wonder if you have allowed insecure thoughts to hinder the grace of God on your life. What if you could live unhindered? **How would your life be different if you stopped trying to please everyone else and started living for the audience of One?**

FREEDOM FROM THE FEAR OF REJECTION

It wasn't long ago that I realized I still had some leftover pain in my life, from years and years ago. I was leading a small group on the topic of freedom, and we spent one session talking about how our past can hinder our future. We really dug deep together in prayer and worship, allowing God to reveal any areas of our lives that were still affected by past pain. And in the middle of that session, in front of my whole group, I broke down. God opened up an old wound that I thought was healed. It wasn't healed; it was suppressed. As memories came rushing back to me, I realized that those old events had an effect on how I lived my life in the present. The rejection that I had experienced as a young person had caused me to live in fear of rejection up to that point. I did an audit of my life, and I could pinpoint decisions that I made in order to avoid rejection. I realized that even the way that I communicated on stage was in order to maintain acceptance from people and avoid any pain from their potential disapproval. But in my attempt to win over people, I wasn't living the freedom God had called me to. **The grace God put on my life was being hindered by my need for approval from man.** Then and there, I decided to pursue freedom from the fear of rejection.

At the end of the group semester, I attended the Freedom Conference in Birmingham, Alabama. The enemy tried to keep me from going and even caused some traffic issues along the way. We pulled into the parking garage two hours late for the conference. I was tempted to go to the hotel instead and start fresh the next day, but I knew something was waiting for me inside that auditorium. And boy, was I right. As soon as I walked in, I could hear the speaker beginning a talk on the fear of rejection. He welcomed up anyone who needed to be free from it, and without hesitation, I marched straight up to the front. A young girl welcomed me up to pray, and I let it all out. I told her I was more than ready for freedom, opened my arms to God, and cried like a baby while she prayed for me. I went back to my seat a different girl. I stood in worship, arms held high, praising God for freedom. After that weekend, I began preaching with a new level of grace, unhindered. I wasn't concerned about what people would think so much. I wasn't questioning myself as much. I got out of the way and allowed God through me. And I can tell you I have noticed a huge difference in my ability to help others.

When you get out of your own way and stop worrying about what people think all the time, you allow God to move freely through you. When you live your life for the audience of One, you become the person He created you to be. And there is so much reward in living that way.

> *Do not throw away your confidence, which has*
> *a great reward.* —*Hebrews 10:35 (ESV)*

So, friend, maybe you need a moment with God to reflect on your past and get really honest with yourself. Are there areas of your life where God's grace is hindered by your pain? If that's the case, it's time for you to have your own freedom conference. Right where you are, turn on some worship music, grab a notebook or journal, and let it flow. Write down those painful memories and how they made you feel. Apologize to God for holding onto that pain that was paid for on the cross. Ask for freedom. Then determine that you will no longer live in slavery to that thought process. You are called to freedom!

Galatians 5:1 (ESV)
For freedom Christ has set us free. Stand firm therefore, and do not submit again to the yoke of slavery.

2 Corinthians 3:17 (ESV)
For the Lord is the Spirit, and wherever the Spirit of the Lord is, there is freedom.

Do an audit of your thought life. How many of your decisions are made based on the opinions and expectations of others?

How would you rate your level of confidence from zero to ten? If it's less than ten, why is that? How would your life be different if you lived with confidence in who God created you to be?

_____

_____

_____

_____

_____

_____

_____

_____

_____

_____

_____

OVER IT

CHAPTER 14

*Therefore, if anyone is in Christ, he is a new
creation. The old has passed away; behold, the
new has come.*—2 Corinthians 5:17 (ESV)

Have you ever been so frustrated with something, or someone, that
you shout, "I'm over it!"? Have you tried to fix a situation, solve an
issue, or deal with a difficult person for so long that you exhaust all
your mental and emotional energy to the place where you're just over it?
My hope for this chapter is to get you to the place where you decide to get
over your old self and on with your new one.

EXPIRED ID

The Bible says we are made new in Christ, and yet, many good Christians
are still walking around with old identities. Labels that were given to them
in grade school still reside in their head. Words that were spoken over
them by parents, coaches, teachers, and relatives still hinder who they
are today. Pain from past experiences causes them to put up walls around

their heart in order to protect them from future hurt. In the last couple chapters, we dealt with critics (Eliabs) and embraced our uniqueness. Now, it's time to redefine who we are and find confidence for our calling!

I know this process well because I've been through it. And it took me a long time of soul-searching to realize that I was still allowing old identities to affect who I was as an adult. It hindered my personality, my sense of humor, my conversations, and my pursuit of the calling on my life. I lived in constant state of undue pressure. Before speaking, I would over-rehearse for fear of messing up. And after speaking, I would beat myself up over and over again over little things I shouldn't have said. This wasn't just when I spoke in front of crowds. It was all the time. Every time I left a conversation, I would immediately feel bad about something I said. I would overthink it and exaggerate the effect it may have had on that person. The truth was, that person wasn't thinking about me. They had moved on to the next thing in their day, and I was wasting time and energy being worried about little things that didn't matter.

Then one day, I got over it. I was through with the pressure. It was time for a new view of myself. I began to believe something crazy. I started living as if everyone I met loved me. Everyone. My neighbors. My coworkers. My friends. My congregation. The groups I speak to. Everyone. I lived with the naive thought process that they all loved me. But what if they didn't? So what!? I would rather live my life believing that everyone loves me than always be trying to figure out which ones don't. I have found that I treat people better. I smile a lot more. I walk a little taller. And I live with more confidence. I think we can all benefit from a bit more confidence. Don't believe me? Take it from the master conversationalist, Les Giblin:

> *"We used to think that the trouble with the egotists was that they thought too highly of themselves... We now know, without a doubt, that the self-centered, egotistical person is not suffering from too much self-esteem, but too little."*
> —Les Giblin, The Art of Dealing with People

Many people believe that the problem with the world is that people are self-centered and conceited and they need correction, discipline, and criticism. But what if the exact opposite is true? What if they really need someone to encourage them? What if they really need to know their worth? What if they never had anyone speak life-giving words over them? I happen to believe that everyone could benefit from a dose of confidence, because when we're more secure in who we are, we are more apt to focus on helping others.

This chapter and the next are going to work together to help you...

Get over yourself and get on with your calling!

We are going to get over our failures, our shortcomings, our past, our guilt, our anger, and our old labels, and get on with the God-given calling on our lives with confidence!

IT'S NOT ABOUT YOU

You could say that Simon Peter was one of Jesus' BFFs. Jesus had hundreds of followers who learned from him, twelve chosen disciples, and three close men who got to experience Him on a deeper level. Peter was one of those three. Peter was also the one who proclaimed Jesus as the Messiah by the power of the Holy Spirit, and was given his new name, Petros (aka "the rock"), based on this revelation that Jesus was the Son of God. Jesus said, "Upon this rock I will build my church, and the gates of hell shall not prevail against it" (Matthew 16:18). But Peter wasn't perfect. When times got tough, he gave in to peer pressure and denied knowing Jesus. He chose his own life over his faith. He had promised to stand beside Jesus even unto death, but then gave up on that promise when Jesus was on trial. After Jesus' death and resurrection, you can imagine the guilt that Peter experienced. Feeling like a failure, he went back to being Simon the fisherman, giving up on his calling as a disciple.

We can all relate to Peter. We've all messed up in relationships. We've all said things we wish we could take back. We've all made mistakes. And if we aren't careful, we can allow the guilt of those mistakes to define us. We can begin to believe that we are no good. We are not worthy of great things. We might as well go back to living our old life because we can't make it in this new one. But how wrong and how selfish would that be? Let's see how Jesus dealt with this thought process.

> When they had finished breakfast, Jesus said to Simon Peter, "Simon, son of John, do you love me more than these?" He said to him, "Yes, Lord; you know that I love you." He said to him, "Feed my lambs." [16] He said to him a second time, "Simon, son of John, do you love me?" He said to him, "Yes, Lord; you know that I love you." He said to him, "Tend my sheep." [17] He said to him the third time, "Simon, son of John, do you love me?" Peter was grieved because he said to him the third time, "Do you love me?" and he said to him, "Lord, you know everything; you know that I love you." Jesus said to him, "Feed my sheep."
> —John 21:15–17

I think it's amazing that Jesus gave Peter three opportunities to proclaim his love and devotion, offering him redemption from the three times he denied him. Jesus uses Peter's old name, Simon, to address him in this moment, knowing that Peter is feeling more like an ordinary fisherman than a great disciple. And in this interaction, Jesus explains two very important things we can all learn from.

The first is this: it's not about you. When God calls you to something, He knows you are going to mess up. He knows He has called an imperfect person. He knows your areas of weakness. But that doesn't stop Him, and it shouldn't stop you. Your calling is not about you; it's about His sheep, His people. The moment you start to walk backward, away from your calling, because you think you aren't good enough, is the moment you let selfishness win. How selfish it is to think that your security is more important than the people you are called to reach. There are lost sheep out there waiting for you to fulfill your destiny. Jesus explained three times to

Peter that he was called to tend to God's sheep, feed them (the gospel), and tend to them when Jesus went back to the Father.

The second thing Jesus wanted to get across to Peter was this: I'm already over it, and it's time you should be too. Jesus wasn't holding Peter's sin over his head. He wasn't turning a cold shoulder or holding a grudge. He was over it! And it was time that Peter got over it too.

What have you been holding onto, allowing you to feel guilty or ashamed? **God is over it and it's time that you are too.** Maybe you need to take a moment to put the book down and really think about how this applies to you. This topic is worth some soul-searching.

If we are going to receive our new identity in Christ and get on with our calling, we have got to get over our:
- Past
- Guilt
- Flaws
- Unforgiveness
- Anger

If we allow these things to reside within our souls, we will never step into our calling with the confidence and boldness required.

When I was a child, I had a favorite stuffed animal named Scruffy. He was a raccoon from Cedar Point. He went everywhere with me and snuggled with me at night. When Scruffy was nearly decapitated, I took a needle and thread and sewed his head back on. I loved him dearly. But there came a time for Scruffy to get boxed up and left in the past. I had grown up and no longer needed a stuffed animal at my side. Sadly, today many people are walking around with old identities they were given as children. They still allow those labels and harsh words to define them. They are living with expired IDs and until they decide to get over it and get on with their new identity in Christ, they will never know true freedom! They will never see the side of them that was meant for a great purpose. And worst of all, the world will never get to know the real them.

If that's you today, I want you to pray this prayer:

> *Lord, you are a good Father. You have chosen me to do great things for your glory. The world has hurt me, labeled me, and attempted to define me, but I'm over it. Forgive me for listening to the voice of men over your voice. I am ready to receive the identity you gave me from before my birth. Help me to see myself the way you see me. Help me to walk with confidence and boldness. Help me to pursue the things you have called me to. I am a new creation in Christ. The old life has passed away, the new has come, and I am walking in that newness today! In Jesus' name, Amen.*

GRACE STORY **SURVIVING ROCK BOTTOM**
Bennett Smith

He keeps saving me over and over again. That's not a theological statement; it's a literal one. He's done it my whole life. For the longest time I couldn't figure out why.

I was born in Alameda County, California, in 1964 after He convinced my mother in her car (on the way to abort me) to trust Him with my life. My alcoholic dad had beaten her while she was pregnant with my sister Sabrina, and she was born with health issues as a result. She only lived about a year. Shortly after that, my mom became pregnant with me and simply felt that she could not endure that kind of pain again and thought it would be better not to bring me into this world. She scheduled the appointment, but by the grace of God, she didn't show up. That's how my personal story began.

There are a number of other times in my early years that He seemed to intervene miraculously to spare me. It gave me the illusion that I was bulletproof. I've since discovered the truth that it has absolutely nothing to do with me. If you could watch my life on a screen like a movie, I'm convinced you would think at certain points, "There's no way that this

guy will ever amount to anything positive. Guys like that don't change."
Then, if you could watch how I served God passionately for over 25 years,
you would see how inspiring it was that I beat those odds and appeared
to have "made it" as the lead pastor of a successful, growing, life-giving
church. Then, you would have been shocked as you watched me fall and
lose everything that had ever been important to me, starting with my
mother.

After my mother died, in 2011, my life took a downward spiral. I began
to respond differently to people and circumstances than I ever had before,
resulting in conflict, pain, separation, and alienation from the people I
had loved. They say a mama's prayers are powerful, and I now see how
important her prayers were to me for many years, but once she passed, I
went into a dark place. I was no longer bulletproof. My poor choices led
to failures in many areas. My marriage of twenty-nine years failed, my
relationship with my five kids was greatly damaged, and I was no longer
fit to serve the church I had loved and led for over twenty years. I lost
hope and was drowning out the pain with alcohol, which led to a loss of
control, anger, and poor choices. I had become a failure, and worse yet, a
"moral failure." It was plastered all over the media. Everyone I loved got a
front-row seat to my self-destruction. My life was shattering into a million
pieces, and there was no way to piece it back together.

If you knew me then, you would have completely agreed with me that
I was never coming back from such a long, hard fall. But somehow,
God got through to me at my friend's condo in North Myrtle Beach in
October of 2013. In my heart I knew what He was saying to me: "I know
it feels like the end to you and you cannot imagine a preferred future at
this moment, but you can still write the end of your story by my grace."
It's like He showed me my life up to that moment, and I could see that
He had ALWAYS been there with me through everything, way before I
even knew that He was. I felt like He asked me to answer a question in
my own heart in light of all He had already done for me. Did I really
want my story to end right then with the words…"And then he died, the
end"? He knew how to get to me because He made me this way. I just
couldn't quit on Him because He never quit on me.

So I went home and survived a living hell (much of which was self-induced) by His grace, while surrounded by His love and mercy. He never left my side. He held my hand and loved me right on through it all. I've learned that I can endure anything because I know He's WITH ME, even when I'm far less than perfect. My ugliness doesn't scare Him away. Things are a lot better now. I am beginning to see a new chapter unfold in my story. I can see a new purpose for my life, and it's given me fresh energy and passion for serving Him again. I'm looking forward to seeing how my story will end and bringing Him the honor and glory He deserves.

SCRIPTURE STUDY:

MATTHEW 16:18 (ESV)
And I tell you, you are Peter, and on this rock I will build my church, and the gates of hell shall not prevail against it.

JEREMIAH 1:5
Before I formed you in the womb I knew you, and before you were born I consecrated you; I appointed you a prophet to the nations.

JOURNAL PROMPTS:

What old labels have you allowed to define you? Have there been words spoken over you, about you, or to you that have affected how you see yourself?

What does God say about you in that area?

What do you need to get over in order to receive the new identity God is offering you?

_____

_____

_____

_____

_____

_____

_____

_____

_____

_____

ON WITH IT

CHAPTER 15

But one thing I do: forgetting what lies behind
and straining forward to what lies ahead.
—Philippians 3:13 (ESV)

N ow that we have gotten over ourselves, it is time to get on with our calling. I love how Apostle Paul puts it in Philippians 3:13. We have forgotten what lies behind, and now it is time press on forward toward what lies ahead.

In this chapter, we are going to learn how to have confidence for our call, even in the midst of our mess. Let's start with a little game of "Have You Ever."

- Have you ever responded with "you too" at an inappropriate time? Like when your waiter says, "Enjoy your meal"? Have you ever said "you're welcome" before someone said "thank you"?

- Have you ever yelled at your spouse for losing the keys, only to find them where you left them?

- Have you ever forgotten to pick up your child from a practice, friend's house, or school?

- Have you ever asked when the baby is due only to find out she wasn't pregnant?

- Have you ever tried to get into the wrong car, and ended up looking like a criminal?

- Have you ever walked headfirst into a screen door?

- Have you ever been humiliated on national television?

Just last week (as of the writing this chapter), I received a text from a friend that read: "Did you know you were on Steve Harvey today?" At the time, I was knee-deep in toys, cleaning my basement. I thought for a moment, "I'm right here, how could I have been on national television moments ago?" I told her no, at which point she sent me a link that would completely change the course of my day. I followed the link to find my face as the butt of a joke on national television. The Steve Harvey show had found a video of me getting spit on by a llama and used it as the highlight of their "last laugh" part of the show. Not only did millions of people watch me get spit on, but Steve narrated the whole thing, making me out to be a total ditz, even to the extent of calling me "stupid." Now, let me tell you, years ago I would have been mortified. But this day, I thought it was hysterical. I was so entertained by it. You have to understand my personality. I live for laughs. There are few things I enjoy more than making people chuckle. It makes me smile to make others smile, and seeing the tears of laughter on the faces of his audience was priceless. The point is, we all make mistakes. We all do stupid things. We all do things we regret. But we can't allow little mistakes to keep us from moving forward in the calling God has given us.

> *For all have sinned and fall short of the glory of God.*—Romans 3:23 (ESV)

Do you see that word "all"? That means even that person who appears to be perfect messes up! Even your pastor messes up. Even that super professional executive who seems to live in a suit and tie makes mistakes from time to time. If you are waiting until you're perfect to start pursuing your calling, you better grab a Snickers, friend, because it's going to be a while!

We have got to learn to have confidence even in the midst of our mess.

> *Let us then with confidence draw near to the*
> *throne of grace, that we may receive mercy and*
> *find grace to help in time of need.*
> —*Hebrews 4:16 (ESV)*

It takes confidence to approach God. It takes confidence to walk in faith. It takes confidence to pursue your calling. But you're not going to get confident by waiting until you're perfect. You will never measure up to the standard of perfection. So, how can we walk in confidence when we know what a mess-up we are? By relying on the power of God.

We learned in the last chapter that Peter was given a second chance at his calling of being a disciple. Jesus communicated in three short words—"feed my sheep"—that He had already gotten over Peter's mistake and that Peter's purpose was not about him, it was about the people to which he was called to minister. So, what happened next? Did Peter go back to being a fisherman, or did he leave the past in the past and press on to what was ahead? We can read in the book of Acts that Peter was filled with the Holy Spirit on the day of Pentecost and preached his first sermon, by which three thousand people were saved. He was arrested, brought in front of the religious leaders, and threatened for being so bold.

> *Now when they saw the boldness of Peter and*
> *John, and perceived that they were uneducated,*
> *common men, they were astonished. And they*
> *recognized that they had been with Jesus.*
> —*Acts 4:13 (ESV)*

Peter was still an ordinary man, but with extraordinary boldness. What changed? Did Peter go to Bible school and get a degree so that he could be confident preaching his first sermon? No. Did he buy a new pickup truck that made him feel more like a man? No. Did he get a promotion, with a nice corner office and a bigger paycheck? No. Peter was still an ordinary, uneducated man, but now he was determined to let nothing stop him from pursuing his calling. Jesus had commissioned him to feed the sheep, and no beating or threat on his life was going to stop him. He was fully reliant on the power of God.

Friend, I hope you're getting this. **It is okay to be inadequate and walk confidently.**

MY SECRET

I love a good Marvel movie. I like to imagine that I am the underdog with superhero powers and I have been given the mission of saving the world against the power of the enemy. One of my favorite scenes is near the end of *Avengers: Age of Ultron* when the alien spaceships are destroying the city and the fate of all mankind is on their shoulders. Captain America turns to Bruce Banner and says, "Now would be a good time to get angry." As the debris flies around them, Bruce turns to Captain and says, "That's my secret, Captain. I'm always angry."

My secret, friend, is that I'm always inadequate. I will never measure up to the standard of perfection. I will continue to do and say silly things from time to time. I will mess up. I will fall short. There are some who look at my qualifications and question my call. But I refuse to allow my inadequacies to stop me from pursuing what I know that God has called me to do. He has called me to encourage people, to preach His word, to give hope to the hopeless, and to be an example of Christ's love to a hurting world.

Peter was inadequate, but it didn't stop him. I am inadequate, but it won't stop me. You are inadequate, but that shouldn't stop you from pressing forward into the call of God on your life.

EPHESIANS 4:1–3

I therefore, a prisoner for the Lord, urge you to walk in a manner worthy of the calling to which you have been called, ² with all humility and gentleness, with patience, bearing with one another in love, ³ eager to maintain the unity of the Spirit in the bond of peace.

JOURNAL PROMPTS:

What dream, goal, or desire have you been putting off because you think you're unqualified?

How will that dream or goal help others?

What is one brave step you can take toward that today?

_____

_____

_____

_____

_____

_____

_____

_____

_____

_____

_____

_____

_____

FINISHING THE RACE

CHAPTER 16

Being confident of this, that he who began a
good work in you will carry it on to completion
until the day of Christ Jesus.
—Philippians 1:6 (NIV)

Well, I find it comical and very appropriate that this chapter came when it did. As I sit here writing the final chapter of this book for you, it has been months since I've looked at these pages, or written a single word for this project.

HITTING THE WALL

A few months ago, I hit a wall. Have you ever been there? Have you ever started something with passion and energy, and then a few steps in, found yourself uninspired and ready to quit? Have you acted on a God-given dream, but then when it didn't come to fruition in good time, gave up on it? Have you just gotten tired and allowed life to consume all your time and energy? I get it. Life gets in the way sometimes. For me, it's been the last few months. As I focused my energies on Sunday services, events, investing in my leaders, and taking care of my family, this dream of finishing the race that is this book was placed on the back burner. But recently I heard a sermon from a friend that re-ignited my passion and brought me back into the race. He said, "In life, we can either quit, camp, or climb." (Thanks Pastor Josh.) I hadn't exactly quit on this book; I had just been camping out near the finish line. The truth is, I know what it takes to cross the finish. I know the motivation and energy required to push through those final laps of publishing, and I wasn't feeling it. But God began a good work, and it is His will to see it to completion. **Thank God I'm not in this race alone, and neither are you!**

If God has placed a dream in your heart, it is probably taking longer than you expected. It is probably much harder than you expected it to be. It probably required much more of you than you planned for. You may have thought, "God is just going to wave his magic wand, and poof, it will be done, and it will be amazing!" Then comes months of blood, sweat, and tears, and you find yourself getting frustrated. Well, friend, you're not alone. When I think back to the founders of our faith, the heroes of the Bible, I remember people who were given a promise from God, but it did not pan out exactly as they planned. Abraham waited twenty-five years for his promised son. Moses wandered the wilderness for forty years before reaching the Promised Land. David had a dream to build God a temple. He made the plans and acquired the funds, but it would be his son, Solomon, who would bring it to completion. The Israelites marched around the city of Jericho seven days, and seven times the final day, before the walls came down. Joseph had a dream as a young boy that one day he would lead his brothers, but he had to go through many years of slavery and trials before that day would come. If these people had allowed fatigue, division, or frustration to stop them at lap four, or five, or six, they would never have witnessed the incredible miracle they did that day. **For all these men and women of faith, the journey wasn't easy, but the promise was worth it.**

When God makes a promise, He means it. He doesn't tease His children. He doesn't give you hopes and dreams and only enough resources to make it halfway. He will see it to completion, but it may require some hard work, some long-range planning, and some endurance to see it through. The good news is, if you are willing to do your part, the end result is greater than you could ever predict. The blessing of God never fails. He is a God of great surprises!

> *Now to him who is able to do far more abundantly than all that we ask or think, according to the power at work within us, ²¹ to him be glory in the church and in Christ Jesus throughout all generations, forever and ever. Amen.*
> —*Ephesians 3:20-21*

Every time God has asked me to do something, it has been harder than I expected, but EVERY TIME it's also been more worthwhile than I ever predicted as well. It's like having children. You imagine rainbows and sunshine. Before I had kids, I had all these expectations of how it was going to be. I imagined putting pretty bows in her hair and tossing a football with him in the yard. I imagined lying on a blanket and watching clouds roll by while our dog frolicked through the field nearby. As I sit here, five kids later, I'm surrounded by sticky floors, piles of laundry, half-eaten donuts, naked Barbies that are painted with nail polish (to match the nail polish on the furniture), and shoes! Oh the shoes I find, all over the house! They can never find their shoes when they need them, which I find impossible to believe because they're everywhere! Parenting is harder, much harder, than I ever predicted. I can count on one hand how many clouds I have watched go by. We don't have a dog, because we have a hard enough time raising things with two legs. It's not exactly how I pictured it, but it is so much more rewarding than I ever imagined. I never thought I could love someone as much as I love my kids. I never thought that one simple bad crayon drawing could bring me to tears. I could never have predicted the warmth it would bring my heart to hold them, even as they grow older. I wouldn't trade it for the world. Just like parenting, your race will be harder to run than you thought, but so much more rewarding than you could have imagined!

IT'S NOT OVER YET

Before Jesus came to this earth in the form of a baby in a manger, the world was a mess. God had been silent for four hundred years. God's people must have wondered if the promised Messiah would ever come. They had heard stories of years earlier, when God did miraculous things and spoke through the prophets, but they had seen none of it. Was it really real? Or was this Yahweh God just a fairytale? Some may have lost hope, but the story wasn't over. In their darkest hour, Jesus was born, the Prince of Peace, the Messiah, the Promised King of Israel, the One who would redeem God's people and restore all mankind. Even today, two thousand years later, the story is not over. Jesus will return, and we will be taken to our new home, where there is no darkness, no pain, no death, no sadness. It can be tempting to lose hope that there is a happy ending to our story. It can be tempting to quit on God, or His plans for our life. It can feel like our life will just always be this way. But, friend, your story is not over yet. There is so much more to it!

SECOND WIND

Every God-given dream requires faith and grit, but you are not in this race alone. You have the mighty outstretched hand of God on your side! He is right there with you now. He is tugging on your heart. He is whispering in your ear, "Keep going, we're almost there." He is strengthening your steps. He is breathing a second wind into you. You may not see the invisible finish line, but it's there, closer than you think. God won't give up on you, so friend, don't give up on Him. His plans for you are good, and there is nothing you can do to change them. He knew who he was working with when He made you. He knew you would mess up. He knew you would get tired. He knew you would want to quit. So He crafted the ultimate plan for you.

"I'll give you my Spirit," He says.

"I'll give you my power."

"I'll give you my strength."

"I'll give you my grace, which is sufficient for you, through every trial."

Whatever race you're running, you're not running it alone. You're running with the Author and Finisher of your faith. The Alpha and Omega. The beginning and the end. The one who was, and is, and is to come. He has always been there. He is there with you now, and He will be with you forever and eternity.

God bless you, dear friend. Although we may not be together in this moment, you should know that you have carried me through this process. When I wanted to quit, I thought of you, the reader. When I felt like my work wasn't good enough, I pictured you getting one small nugget of hope or encouragement from this book, and I kept going. You have been with me this whole time, without knowing it, and I pray that you feel my encouragement with you as you run your race in life. I love you. God loves you. Now go out and finish that race of yours!

> *Therefore, since we are surrounded by so great a cloud of witnesses, let us also lay aside every weight, and sin which clings so closely, and let us run with endurance the race that is set before us.*
> *—Hebrews 12:1 (ESV)*

SCRIPTURE STUDY:

1 CORINTHIANS 9:24 (ESV)

Do you not know that in a race all the runners run, but only one receives the prize? So run that you may obtain it.

JOURNAL PROMPTS:

What race are you running?

Imagine the finish line is closer than you think. How can you run with passion and boldness as you finish your race?

_____

_____

_____

_____

_____

_____

_____

_____

_____

_____

_____

_____

_____

_____

_____

_____

GRACE STORIES

The next, and last, section of this book is full of testimonies of God's amazing grace. These people have been through trials and tragedies unimaginable and lived through them by the grace of God. It is my prayer that as you read these stories, you will be inspired as you run your own race.

Thank you to the men and women within these stories. You are my heroes. Your faith stretches me. I am grateful to God for connecting us, and for your bravery in telling your story.

BEATING THE ODDS
Marcy Riffle

Who would have ever thought our beautiful family vacation would turn into a tragedy?

It was a perfect, sunny July day on Lake Cumberland when the houseboat we rented had a massive explosion. Everything was on fire. The six people I love the most in this world—my husband Gary, my two daughters, and my mom, dad, and sister—were all stuck in that cove on the houseboat, surrounded by flames and breathtaking fumes. I remember not knowing if we were going to make it out alive. Then I saw my husband swim up out of the water, and I could tell he was severely burned. He was totally pale, facial hair charred black to his face and skin hanging off of him everywhere. He had been standing a foot away from the explosion. I prayed to God and begged Him to help us get out. I'll never forget the relief I felt once we were all off the lake safe, but then the panic of trying to get to Gary, who was life-flighted two hours away.

I was able to get to him and ride with him on the second helicopter from UK to UC. When we arrived at the ICU burn unit, I was rushed out of the room so they could assess his injuries. There I stood in a cold waiting room, completely alone, wearing only my bathing suit, no shoes, the smell of gas fumes in my hair and still burning my nose, and no phone, because mine had died when we had to jump into the lake. The tears began to flow as I tried to comprehend what had just happened. I couldn't understand how something intended to be fun had turned into this life-threatening situation. After a couple hours, the lead burn doctor came out to give me the diagnosis. Gary had been burned on 51 percent of his body and had severe damage to his lungs from inhaling the fumes and flames. He was in critical condition, not breathing on his own, and the word "death" was used several times. His lungs were the biggest, scariest obstacle. We were told if he got an infection in his lungs in the first three to five days that he would not survive. Not to mention the many surgeries he was facing with grafting for his burns. As I heard the news, I think I was actually numb. Hearing but not fully comprehending. When I first got to see him, he was pretty much unrecognizable. He was swollen, appearing to be about forty pounds heavier, wrapped head to toe in gauze, tubes and wires everywhere, and so many machines keeping him alive. I remember feeling sick as I walked back out to the waiting room to get my teenage daughters to take them back to see their dad. I knew in that moment our lives had changed forever, whether he lived or died. I decided that I needed to hand this whole thing over to God because the circumstances were out of my control. For just a brief moment, I questioned God, asking, "Why did you allow this to happen to us?" But I knew I needed to trust that God had a plan. I prayed for peace for us and a miraculous healing for my husband. I held tight to my faith and hoped I could handle the outcome. It was an agonizing feeling, being so hopeless and waiting minute by minute for updates, praying for no bad news. Then suddenly, I was overwhelmed by a feeling of love and peace, as if prayers were covering me like a blanket. My worry and fear eased up a little, and I felt like I could actually comprehend all the medical information.

Over the days and weeks, our family, friends, and community rallied for us with so many amazing donations of all kinds. Day after day I prayed for healing and kept my faith strong. That healing came! It was so remarkable that the doctors were even shocked and puzzled. After being unable to remember the first two weeks, Gary was finally able to understand what happened. One of the first things he mouthed to me was "We are going to church and we are getting baptized." I agreed. Against all odds, he was able to walk out of the hospital just thirty days after the accident, and with hard work and lots of therapy, he has made an amazing recovery. God had given us a real-life miracle!

As requested, once we got home, we headed to church. We made a decision, as a family, to rededicate our life to God and put Him first. Shortly after, all four of us—myself, Gary, and our two daughters—were water baptized. God works in mysterious ways. Our worst nightmare became the event that saved our lives for eternity!

A FAMILY TRANSFORMED
Kathleen Benis

Life was good. It was the year that my sweet son came running across the street to let me know he accepted Jesus as his savior.

"What? Your dad is a Jew. Your mom a Catholic. Don't you think that's enough religion in our family? Let's go talk with Timothy's mother. She needs to know her son is preaching in their garage."

Well, guess what? I came home saved! Lynn showed me that the love of Jesus and His grace far outweighed the stress I put on myself to be good enough.

This peace was short-lived. Our son, with no previous symptoms, had a psychotic break and was diagnosed at 3:00 a.m. on Mother's Day with bipolar disorder. I soon learned of this enemy who came to kill my dreams, steal my joy, and destroy the opportunities my sweet son had such potential for. When the doctors told me, "You don't get this! He is the worst case we have seen," I felt this Holy Ghost fire rise up in me. I stood up and told them, "I have two choices. First, I will find a Christian doctor. Then, I will take this case to the Most High court!"

I can't say Jesus brought total healing to my son, but I will say He brought people, places, and situations that showed the grace and love of Jesus spilling into our heartbreak. Our family began to heal through the peace and presence of Jesus. We sense His wisdom as we learn to navigate our new normal. We are finding joy in our journey through this Most High God, who is real! If you let Him, He will make himself real to you.

This is the prayer I asked my sweet husband to pray when his heart was breaking over the realities of our son's illness. "Jesus, if you're real, make yourself real to me." Twenty-two years later, Jesus pierced my husband's heart. He became a completed Jew on November 22, 2018. If you let Him, Jesus will complete you too. And you will see the rhythm of His grace.

I WAS BROKE. NOW I'M NOT.
Joe Sangl

I remember December 2, 2002 like it was yesterday. After living in South Carolina for the past four years, my family (my bride, Jenn, and our 4-year old daughter, Melea) had returned to our home state of Indiana with a new job in a new town. We were promptly greeted by eight inches of snow and a temperature of eight degrees.

Upon starting my new job, I learned that my new employer paid their employees once per month, and it would be a few weeks before we would receive income. This exposed a truth I had ignored for several years: Our money was out of control.

We were completely clueless about money management and our financial decisions proved it. The monthly financial gymnastics and hurdles required to pay our bills constantly reminded us of our lack of knowledge. Our list of debts acquired was quite impressive: car loan, truck loan, student loans, credit card balances, furniture loan, mortgage, and we even owed my parents.

On that cold, snowy December day, I decided it was time to find a better way to manage money. My mind raced with several thoughts: "How is this possible?" and "This has got to change!" and "This is embarrassing!" All of these thoughts led me to one big question: "How do I stop, fix, change this ridiculous madness?"

This question sent me on a quest for knowledge. I acquired and read every money book I could get my hands on. It was during this time that I discovered how much money wisdom is found in the Bible. One particular verse stood out to me in the book of Proverbs.

> *"The plans of the diligent lead to profit as surely as haste leads to poverty." – Proverbs 21:5*

As I read this verse, my problem became clear: We didn't have a plan! It's impossible to diligently follow a non-existent plan. We immediately began to view our money differently. It started with a prayer or repentance: "God, we're sorry for mismanaging all of the money you've provided to us."

Then our prayer was one seeking the Lord's guidance: "God, please help us become better at this. We sense a calling in our life, and we recognize that we must get this area of our life in order."

A short while later, I was taking a Sunday afternoon nap when Jenn walked into our living room proudly holding a sheet of paper with numbers hand-written all over it and asked, "What do you think of this budget?" My old inclination to run away from facing our financial reality immediately surfaced, but God, in his grace, enabled us to have our first-ever productive financial conversation.

At that moment, our life, marriage, and money forever changed. We prepared a budget – and this time it worked! Just fourteen months later, we had saved a one month emergency fund and paid off all of our non-house debt: the truck, the car, the credit cards, and even our student loans.

As we rejoiced in our newfound financial freedom, many of our friends began asking for assistance with their money challenges. We began leading financial classes at our church. The classes swiftly grew from a dozen to more than a hundred. Every time we taught, a passion for helping others win with money God's way began to burn deep within me. Every time I helped an individual family or led the class, my passion and burden grew. This passion grew into my life's mission: To help people live fully funded lives being able to do exactly what they've been put on earth to do – regardless of the cost or income potential.

Just four years later, in September 2006, I left Corporate America and joined the pastoral team at a church I had helped plant in Anderson, South Carolina (NewSpring Church). The church had grown to about 6,000 in attendance. The position I took? One especially created to help people win with their money God's way. I wrote and released my first book, "I Was Broke. Now I'm Not.", to share my story and provide practical teaching so others could experience fully funded lives.

In 2009, I Was Broke. Now I'm Not. became it's own independent organization. Since that time, the Lord has blessed us to be able to help more than one million people all throughout the world via live teaching events, books, and financial tools. It is a true blessing to be able to testify to the Lord's work in our lives.

MIRACULOUS HEALING
Sue McDonald

When I was approximately twenty-seven years old, I began to notice the strength in my body wasn't what it should be. After months of testing and not getting any better, I was diagnosed with fibromyalgia. The doctors informed me if my body continued on the path it was on, that I would be wheelchair bound in approximately two years. Mind you, my daughter was only a few years old, and I had gotten to the point I couldn't pick her up any longer. This was about the time my husband, Chris, had surrendered to preach, and our insurance was changing. I was praying one day about what to do about the insurance, and God spoke to me and said, "The healing is yours. Receive it." So that's what I did. I spoke to my body daily and commanded strength to come into it. Every morning before my feet hit the floor, I would say, "Devil, I serve you notice, I am strong! I refuse to bow to weak muscles! God is my strength!" I did that every day for a year, all while confessing to family and friends that God healed me of fibromyalgia. I prayed for others who were instantly healed while I had received my healing by faith, knowing I had it no matter what the facts looked like. I still hurt, I was still exhausted, but I was healed and I knew it.

One day while I was in the kitchen, Chris was chasing Erin through the house and the next thing I knew, she started yelling, "Get me, Mom! Get me!" She had learned that I couldn't just pick her up. But in that moment, something happened. A miracle was in the air. I reached for her as she leaped in my arms and we were all amazed....I had picked her up! I didn't hurt, I wasn't weak...I was healed!! We all laughed, cried, and praised God right there in the kitchen. For one year I confessed healing. I believed it! And I received it in full that day, never to have any symptoms again!

STANDING ON THE WORD
Stephanie Ferner

I was a mom of four, had my own business, and was working twelve-hour days. I was a cheer coach, served my church, and had a flourishing life. In the years leading up to this, I had left an abusive marriage, where I barely escaped alive. I had been through so much mental turmoil that I believed I couldn't handle any more. During this season, I had rededicated myself to the Lord, got baptized, and was strengthening my relationship with God.

One day my health declined. I went from being an active cheer coach to lying in a hospital bed for months. The doctors advised me to file for disability and told me that I wouldn't be able to care for my children or drive again. I couldn't walk to the restroom alone. I was diagnosed with a lifelong illness with no cure or FDA-approved medication. When I thought things couldn't get any worse, I developed blood clots in my lungs at twenty-eight years old. My precious children had to go live with family. I slipped into a state of depression and started doubting God. My anxiety was so bad, I was scared to move. I would lie in my bed for weeks at a time, too sick or weak to eat. It was then that I decided that I had nothing to lose, and I started believing I was ALREADY healed. Every day I would pray and thank God. I started to believe that He would use my trial for my testimony. Within three weeks from that day, I was able to walk and drive! I got my kids back shortly after! Life was returning to normal, but I still didn't have money to pay my bills and almost lost my home and vehicle. Instead of looking for a job, I did the UNTHINKABLE! I prayed that God would take care of my finances. The following Monday, I was offered a job working from home making more than I was before…by a complete stranger! While I am still sick, I am beating all of the odds that the doctors gave me, because I believed in God's word, not the world's.

MOMENTS
Rhonda Slark

It was six years ago. I sat beside her bed, wondering, "How do I say goodbye?" This is the woman who gave me life and sacrificed herself daily to give me the very best she possibly could. The gracious, loving, and giving lady whom everyone thought of so highly. The kind of person you wanted to become, yet, a very simple, non-assuming lady who never put herself above anyone else. There were so many things I needed to say, but inside I was screaming. "Please, you can't leave me! I still need you! Who is going to be here to help me?"

Several days earlier, my mom, my very best friend in the world, had become very ill. After just a few days, the diagnosis came. "Severe pulmonary fibrosis," the doctor stated. "There is nothing we can do to save her. She is dying; you only have days." I did not leave her side. I could not, for fear that she would not be breathing when I returned. As her time neared, we talked of everything. I wanted to ensure she knew just how much she really meant to me. I asked her everything I needed to ask. Was she afraid? Could I do anything? I let her know I was so proud that she was MY mommy and how much she meant to me. I told her that if I became just a fraction of the woman she was, I would be successful. I watched her as she weakened, every day, every hour, almost every minute, a little more.

I noticed on Saturday morning that there was a distinct change. She could no longer respond. Her facial expressions had become very strained, and she looked as if she were gasping for every breath. The nurses convinced me that this is part of the way our bodies begin to shut down and she was not suffering. I absolutely could not take it anymore. I excused myself and quietly went to the hospital's chapel. Thankfully, no one was in there. I found myself in the wee hours of the morning on my face before God begging Him to not let her die struggling. I don't know how long I was there, but the silence of the chapel was broken with my sobs which turned into screams, begging for her life. I knew that unless there was an absolute miracle, her time was very limited but I could not bear for her to die like this. After a few minutes I was able to compose myself and return to the

Palliative Care unit.

My dad and I sat quietly for most of the day. My dad, my hero, the strongest man in the world, seemed so small. This heartbroken man sobbed and asked God to please take him with her. He had been in love with her since the day he met her in 1960. His world was falling apart, yet the silence of the room seemed to be comforting. Many friends, pastors, and family members stopped in to say their goodbyes.

When they all had left, a quiet settled over the room. In my heart I kept reminding God of my request. Dad and I were the only two people in the room, and I had my head resting on her hand softly, crying. There had been no response from her for twenty-four hours, nothing, not even a movement of her arms or legs. As I was lying there, I felt a movement and sat straight up. My mom, who had not been able to even lift her head up for days, sat straight up in the bed, eyes wide open with a smile on her lips, held her right hand up in the air as though she were reaching for something unseen by us, and immediately lay her head back on her pillow with the most peaceful, relaxed look she had had in days. Even though her heart continued to beat for a few hours longer, I believe it was that moment she stepped into the arms of Jesus. I cannot humanly describe the peace that filled the room when Dad and I woke up (at exactly the same moment) in the wee hours of the morning and realized her heart had stopped. Even the physician that came in said she had never, in all her career, felt that kind of palpable peace. My brother, sister-in-law, Dad, and I sat in that peaceful room with her for several hours until we felt we could leave. Those were moments I have grown to treasure.

God answered the prayer of this heartbroken little girl. Yes, I am a grown woman, but in that moment, I was a little girl again who just needed to know that God was still listening and that He truly cared. In the midst of my sorrow and brokenness, God wrapped His arms around me. I felt, at that moment, that God himself was crying with me. In the days, weeks, months, and now years that have followed, I have come to cherish those precious last days and moments with her. More than anything, I am thankful for the dying grace that God gave to me and my family during those moments. Dying grace—I had heard of it all my life, but now it had become alive to me. Writing this I feel every emotion as though it were happening today. I never want to forget those feelings. My prayer is that I will make every moment count and make my mom proud of her daughter until I see her again.

THE LIGHTHOUSE
Sara Heistand

Two days before Thanksgiving 2010, I walked out of my home in Columbus with nothing more than a few garbage bags of my children's clothing. I was so afraid as I left my abusive husband, but I will never forget the feeling I had as I drove toward the domestic violence shelter in Lancaster. The feeling of pure freedom. The weight that had been crushing me was finally lifted, and I could breathe for the first time in years. That feeling didn't last long and was quickly replaced with the anxiety, fear, and loneliness. My closest family was over three hours away, and I had just a few local friends.

That first night at the Lighthouse is forever imprinted on my mind. The ladies there were so kind and caring. My three children (ages seven, five, and eighteen months) and I had our own private room and bathroom. Looking back, it was the only thing that gave me any sense of dignity in those days. I was so ashamed that I had no money to buy food for my children. We went two days with barely anything to eat before I finally asked for help. I was so alone and broken that I lay sobbing on my bathroom floor. I was exhausted and scared, alone and afraid. I had to be strong for my children, but inside I was terrified. I had no idea how I would manage to support three young children on my own with no income and no place to live.

One week after arriving at the shelter, I discovered that I was pregnant with my fourth child. Unfortunately, I began miscarrying the baby on Christmas Eve. I had to have a D&C to complete the miscarriage. I was a junior at the Mount Carmel College of Nursing in Columbus at the time, but at this point the stress and depression of leaving an abusive marriage, discovering an unexpected pregnancy, and enduring a miscarriage with no support from anyone led me to my breaking point. I withdrew from nursing school to focus on my children.

Then came the light at the end of the tunnel. I befriended another woman at the shelter named Candi. She started taking me to church with her, and it was here that I finally found hope for my future. I finally discovered who I am. I found that the love I had always been missing in my life was always there; He was always with me! I immersed myself in building my relationship with God.

I spent a total of three months living in the shelter with my children. During that time, God provided me with a job and a new apartment for myself and my children. I went back to school and got a degree in nursing, and I've been a registered nurse now for nine years. Aside from raising my kids, it is my greatest joy to take care of patients and be an encouragement to them. I still look back on those times as some of the toughest of my life, but now I can see that God was always there, and He used that experience (and Candi) to bring me back to a relationship with Him.

THE MYTH OF PRINCE CHARMING
Rachel Dawn

"'And they lived happily ever after' is one of the most tragic sentences in literature. It's tragic because it's a falsehood. It is a myth that has led generations to expect something from marriage that is not possible." —Joshua Lievman

Once upon a time, long long ago, in a bedroom not-so-far away, you, as a little girl, were told a bedtime story of a Prince who would come for you, sweep you off your feet, and rescue you from your ordinary life and all the wrong guys you would date. You would exchange your vows at the wedding of your dreams and ride off into the sunset on horseback to live happily ever after.

That story was then reiterated through every movie you ever saw, every book you ever read, every magazine article ever published, and even every youth group meeting you ever attended.

The only problem with riding off into the sunset is that after the sun sets, and night falls, morning the next day comes. And this person who you thought was perfect wakes up with morning breath and bed head, leaves his underwear on the bathroom floor, squeezes your toothpaste tube the wrong way, leaves the toilet seat up, and then saunters into the kitchen expecting you to produce a hot breakfast.

Months like this go by and each night he comes home from work, expects you to have cooked again, and then sits down to watch ESPN highlights or surf the internet rather than doing the things he promised you he would get done around the house.

Reality hits and disenchantment sets in as you realize this was not at all the fairytale you imagined.

Does this sound familiar to you?

This excerpt comes from Chapter 7 of my book, *Now What? A Story of Broken Dreams and the God Who Restores Them.* I titled that chapter "The Myth of Prince Charming," and accurately so. This little girl was me; I had bought the Disney fairytale dream hook, line, and sinker. And I paid dearly for it. I wanted to set Walt Disney's gravestone on fire!

After I married my Prince Charming at a young age, it didn't take long at all before reality failed to align with fantasy. By age twenty-five, I found myself divorced and totally disenchanted with the entire idea of marriage. But, four years after that, when my boyfriend proposed, I was forced to revisit my thoughts on white dresses and picket fences.

The night of our engagement, I ordered sixteen books on marriage, divorce, and remarriage. I resolutely set on a journey to understand what went wrong with my first marriage, so I could avoid another stroke-of-midnight-unraveling-of-my-dreams moment a second time.

What I learned on my journey toward remarriage is, marriage isn't designed to make us happy at all! That's not even the point! The point of marriage is to love another person into the fullness of who God created them to be, to grow ourselves in the same manner, and to show other people Jesus through our example.

It's humanly impossible for another person to make, and keep, me happy for the rest of my life.

And it wasn't until I had that revelation for myself, and adjusted my own expectations accordingly, could I ever begin to be happy in marriage.

My whole life I had been told that for marriages to be successful, they have to have "Jesus at the center of them," but no one ever explained what the heck that meant.

What I discovered through my study was that:

1. Jesus is my source for happiness and contentment, not my husband.

2. Putting God at the center of my marriage means living out Christ-like behavior toward my spouse every day, and unconditionally loving them, even when they're at their ugliest.

Can we all agree, that's WAY easier said than done?!

But it goes back to being filled up by God first. I can only do that if I get filled up with God's love first, then can I pour it back out to Barry.

Every time I get hurt or disappointed by my husband, I remind myself that I, too, am imperfect. And I need grace. I make mistakes and hurt people. I hurt and disappoint God. But when I do, every time—every single time—without exception, no matter how far I went or how wrong I was, God invites me lovingly back into His arms with grace. Passionate grace. More than that, when I am running away from Him in my actions and deeds, He chases after me! That's love.

And I believe what we are called to do is to exemplify that love back into our marriages.

It's been years since that dreaded day when my fairytale dreams were crushed, and I wondered if my life would ever be the same. It certainly has not. It's better than I could ever hope for or imagine! God's grace has enabled me to build a Christ-like marriage with Barry for the last five years, and we are blessed with opportunities to help others create loving marriages that last!

#BROCKSTRONG
Kristi Johnson

Faith is easy when everything is going well in your life. It gets tough when things are heartbreaking or do not make sense. For me, that time came when I lost a huge light in my life, my fourteen-year-old son, Brock. Brock was born with major chronic, unspecific health problems. Which means, on the outside he looked normal and great, but on the inside he had some not-so-good things going on with his blood counts. Despite numerous hospital stays and monthly all-day treatments, he lived a normal, active life. He was super smart and excelled at any sport that he tried. Brock loved Jesus. He invited everyone to church and even had the honor of helping to baptize several of his friends. Brock's medical condition led to him needing a bone marrow transplant. Brock did well early on post-transplant, but then seemed to get infection after infection. He stayed so strong and held to Jeremiah 29:11 and believed that come what may, this was God's plan. Eight months after the transplant, Brock passed away from an infection in his lungs.

To say that I was devastated was the understatement of all times. In spite of having a child with chronic, life-threatening medical issues, my life had been pretty good. I am married to my best friend and high school sweetheart, who is an awesome godly man, and we had two beautiful babies! God and church have always been a huge part of our lives. Having been in the same church since he was born, Brock had people praying for him his entire life! Throw in family, social media, and the impact Brock had on everyone he met—there were literally thousands of people praying for him. I always believed 100 percent that God was going to come in and heal him. Brock was such a mystery to the medical world that I believed God would heal him and get the glory. Well, on May 20, 2015, he didn't. The biggest prayer of my life was blatantly NOT answered.

At first I was just shocked and stood in disbelief. How could everything that I believed in be proven wrong in an instant? I was mad. I was sad. I felt let down. Let down by God. At Brock's memorial service (attended by over four thousand people), I got a glimpse of the impact that God had through this amazing kid on so many people in just fourteen and a half years. So many people who had started believing in God, attending church, and praying because of Brock. We knew that we had to carry on the good that God was doing through him and knew that God would lead us to what that meant. My faith in God and His promise of forever is what helped me put one foot in front of the other every day. We created the BrockStrong foundation, which has had a huge impact on so many people. It would have been easy to stay in bed and go into a depression, but I knew that would not honor Brock or God. I am still here for a reason—God is not done with me! Because He stayed with me during the hardest days of my life, I will spend my days honoring Him through showing people Christ-like (and Brock-like) love through the foundation.

YOUR STORY HERE!

These stories were so inspiring and faith-building! I pray they brought you comfort, hope, and encouragement to keep running your race!

If you have a grace story of your own, I'd love to hear it! Find me on Facebook, or email me your story at **Mindy@impactcity.tv.**

CPSIA information can be obtained
at www.ICGtesting.com
Printed in the USA
LVHW110048030520
654903LV00004B/953

9 781798 561744